AN INTRODUCTION TO
EXPLORATION ECONOMICS
3rd Edition

AN INTRODUCTION TO EXPLORATION ECONOMICS
3rd Edition

Robert E. Megill

PennWell Books

PennWell Publishing Company
Tulsa, Oklahoma

Copyright © 1988 by
PennWell Publishing Company
1421 South Sheridan Road/P. O. Box 1260
Tulsa, Oklahoma 74101

Library of Congress Cataloging-in-Publication Data

Megill, R.E.
　Exploration economics/Robert E. Megill.—3rd ed.
　　p. cm.
　Bibliography: p.
　Includes index.
　ISBN 0-87814-331-9: $59.95
　　1. Prospecting—Economic aspects.　2. Petroleum.　I. Title.　　　　88-2317
TN271.P4M436　　1988　　　　　　　　　　　　　　　　　　　　　　　　CIP
338.4'76221828—dc19　　　　　　　　　　　　　　　　　　　　　　　　(Rev.)

Printed in the United States of America

1　2　3　4　5　92　91　90　89　88

Contents

Preface

Exploration economics does not exist as a separate branch of either academic or practical economics.

It is a strange mixture of engineering economics, mathematics and statistics, probability theory and the more normal sciences of exploration—geology and geophysics. There are textbooks which cover each aspect. Nowhere, however, can one find a reasonable starting point encompassing the economics of the search for hydrocarbons. This book is a starting point. It is not a scholarly text on economics; it is a resumé of practical evaluating knowledge written especially for the working explorationist and the student geologist.

The book is written for the explorationist who knows little about the subject and who has forgotten most of his college math. It is intended to be truly introductory. As such the accomplished investment analyst will find this work elementary. He will find certain illustrations which oversimplify or generalize. However, some oversimplification must occur in a primer. Each generalization is footnoted with proper cautions if needed. None of the simplifications suggested will hinder sound investment evaluation.

It is my hope that the interested reader will continue his search amid available literature. The bibliography included at the end of each chapter should assist in that search.

The first edition of *An Introduction to Exploration Economics* was published in 1971. The second edition, published in 1979, included significant additions and brought the text up to date through the tax laws of 1978. Since 1978, three major tax laws have been passed by Congress with changes in depreciation rates, basic tax rates and the elimination of the investment tax credit. The third edition brings the text up to date through the tax laws of 1987. It includes two new chapters, a glossary, and list of acronyms. One of the new chapters deals with the subject of minimum rate of return—or guideline rate of return as it is sometimes called. The other chapter briefly discusses choosing a computer program for economic evaluations.

Significant revisions and changes have been made to the chapters in the third edition. The changes stem from questions asked in teaching both risk analysis and exploration economics as well as from writing and research the author has done since the last edition was published.

No one can write a textbook involving tax laws and government regulations and expect it to remain up to date for long. With the vast increase in regulations streaming forth from both the state and Federal levels, only history will determine what unforeseen changes will affect the accuracy of the third edition. However, the basic principles of cash flow analysis, present value concepts and optimum investment selection remain the same, regardless of changes in tax laws or tax rates. One only need calculate the effect of the changes on the cash flow stream for a prospect or play (or any investment) and the effect on all yardsticks can be shown. Thus, even though laws and regulations may change, the basic principles in this manual will serve the analyst well because it contains methods and concepts independent of such changes.

New problems (and the answers to these problems) have been added to help the reader understand the concepts presented. By working problems we gain an idea of how clear our understanding is of what is presented. Successfully working the problems indicates a clear understanding of concepts conveyed.

To all who read this new edition, may it help you in your search for a better understanding of what it takes to select the best among numerous investment opportunities.

Robert E. Megill
Kingwood, Texas

Acknowledgments

Every author incurs debts of assistance in his publications. In the first edition of *An Introduction to Exploration Economics* the author is indebted to Messrs. Paul Costa, Frank Sisti and G. Rogge Marsh for substantial contributions. In addition, Messrs. Frank Holmesly, Harold Ranzau and Fred Heidner read selected chapters and provided their insights. Mr. R.W. Garrett and Mr. D.P. Meagher read the entire first manuscript and their comments were appreciated. My sincere thanks to Mrs. Vera Dunlop and all the others who helped.

The second edition of *Exploration Economics* owed new expressions of gratitude to Mr. Bob Dreyling, Mr. Trent Meadors, and Mr. E.C. Capen who made significant suggestions. For both the second and third editions my largest debt belongs to Mr. G. Rogge Marsh. Chapters 9, 10 and Appendix D owe much to his ideas and thoughts. His constant encouragement was sometimes the necessary ingredient when the burdens of writing seemed insurmountable.

The third edition benefits from and includes ideas developed since retirement from Exxon in 1984. Many of these ideas were initially expressed in my monthly column in the *Explorer*, a monthly publication of the American Association of Petroleum Geologists (AAPG).

It is my sincere hope that each person who contributed to any of the three editions will feel his efforts were rewarded by this book.

A Word to the Reader

Throughout this textbook two symbols are used to denote either thousands or millions. They are:

$$M = 1,000$$
$$\overline{M} = 1,000,000$$

1 Setting the Stage

If you want to know something about the practical economics of the search for hydrocarbons, the pages which follow will provide a beginning. To become an expert in the analysis of exploratory opportunities will require much more reading—and some practical experience in evaluating plays and prospects. One can, however, acquire new knowledge from the writings and experiences of others, accepting or rejecting parts as desired.

Objectives

To transmit new knowledge by means of the written word, one must have reasonable objectives in mind. The objectives sought here are:

1. To explain the expanding role of economics in the life of the explorationist.
2. To develop a knowledgeable vocabulary of the terms associated with economic analysis.
3. To review the procedures used in preparing economic analyses, and
4. To relate the new vocabulary and knowledge to some specific analyses.

In general the objectives, if achieved, will do more to help you understand economic evaluations than to enable you to prepare them. You should learn when such evaluations can help you; and having requested an evaluation, you will better understand what is received.

We will mention the role of the computer in today's evaluation methods. Its role is a vital one. Much of what is done today in investment evaluation would be impossible without the computer. Nevertheless, you need to know nothing about computers to derive benefits from this manual. Furthermore, none of the problems requires a computer for solution.

Finally, many of the concepts discussed are common to any type of investment analysis. You will find applications to any area of your life where financial decisions are required.

Your Working Environment

Whether you work for a major, complex organization, in a business partnership or are self-employed, economics is in your future.

If you make your livelihood searching for hydrocarbons, this statement is especially true. The explorationist's work begins at the raw material end of a long investment chain (which ends with gasoline in his tank). If his efforts are successful, profits are made possible for many other downstream investments. The exploratory efforts conducted within a major integrated oil company provide investment opportunities for other departments nearer the product end of the investment chain. To begin with, think of your work as contributing to the investment chain.

The first sale of hydrocarbons comes after the development of a property. Thus, the economic success of an exploration program can only be determined after its discoveries are developed and put on production. Exploration economics is in fact the financial consequences of both exploration and production investments—but is related to the time of the exploratory decision.

In a large oil company, the operating departments (exploration, production, marketing, refining, etc.) make the major capital investments. Competition for funds exists between departments. Each department wants money to make investments within its jurisdiction.

Selecting the Best Investment Opportunity

With competition for funds, the selection of the best investments becomes a constant process for management. The selection is not always easy. Investments in different departments have:

1. Different tax considerations.
2. Varying degrees of uncertainty and risk.
3. Interfunctional differences in capital requirements, cash flow characteristics, etc.

Management decisions involving investment opportunities are influenced by various analysis groups. In a few large companies, most functions have an analysis group within their department. In other companies analysis work is completely centralized. Regardless of the location, these groups provide background evaluations for budget purposes and as an added tool for investment decision making. In any business, large or small, selecting the right investments is the key to growth and prosperity. The principles reviewed in this book should help you select the best available investments.

The Decade Ahead for the Oil and Gas Industry

A brief look ahead will serve to illustrate why economic considerations are in your future.

The problems of the next decade will impose needs for careful scrutiny of all investments—including exploration investments. Many of the factors influencing future investments are beyond the control of the explorationist. Yet, some are so critical that their economic consequence must continually be tested. Let us consider several factors.

Interfuel Competition

Because the consumer constantly searches for the best product at the lowest cost, we have interfuel competition. In the history of the petroleum industry we have had conditions of both surplus and shortage. The industry passed through its most unprecedented boom in the 1979–1982 period. This unusual peak of activity was caused by the highest prices in the history of the petroleum industry—almost a twelvefold increase in the wellhead price for crude oil in about a decade. At the peak, prices for crude oil edged toward $40 per barrel and a few natural gas contracts were signed at $10 per thousand cubic feet (Mcf).

The higher prices for oil and gas at the wellhead produced equally high product prices; and the petroleum industry was astonished to find a much greater sensitivity to price than expected and demand began to fall. Lower demand, worldwide, coupled with increased production forced prices lower. As has been true for most of the history of the industry, as an upward price cycle ended, interfuel competition returned with a vengeance.

Projections of supply during the mid-1980s indicated adequate supplies of crude oil for a decade or more. Unless there is a major disruption in supplies from the Middle East, it will be some time before crude prices can increase much beyond the level of inflation.

During the next decade interfuel competition will be fierce. Much depends on the actions of OPEC cartel, whose membership includes most countries in the Middle East, Libya, Nigeria, Venezuela, etc. Any price forecast made in the 1980s falls victim to the actions of OPEC. With Saudi Arabia providing the role of swing producer, OPEC can control the price of crude oil as long as it is willing to restrict production. Most cartels find restrictions of production difficult, as the Saudis have learned. Nevertheless, minimal cooperation among OPEC nations will give the cartel effective control over the worldwide price of crude oil, especially after the year 2000.

Natural gas is not excluded from interfuel competition, as producers of natural gas learned in the mid-1980s. Competition with fuel oil, as boiler fuel, and gas competing with other gas from different areas of the country and world, for example Canada, clearly demonstrates that interfuel competition directly affects prices of natural gas.

Even in conditions of tight supply, the competition between fuels will still exist. The competition between fuels places a ceiling on prices. The ceiling is a relative one that could be affected by general price changes. Consider some of the alternate fuels for crude oil and natural gas.

Shale Oil

Potential shale oil competition is of particular interest. Abundant supplies are available (meaning that no risk is involved in the search). The technology is already available to obtain petroleum products from the kerogen in oil shales of the continental U.S. Crude oil prices might rise under conditions of extremely tight supply. But even if they do, the price can rise only to the point where shale oil becomes an attractive alternate investment. As of now commercial shale oil production is sensitive to:

- crude price
- mining and retorting costs
- tax considerations
- governmental factors affecting the policy on public lands
- disposal of shale wastes

At some time in the future, the right combination of change in these factors will make shale oil deposits economic. At present, the uncertainties associated with each factor preclude an accurate estimate of when this will occur.

Tar Sands

Much the same logic applies to tar sands. Although uneconomical today, tar sands represent potential sources for petroleum products. The deposits being mined in Canada indicate that the technology is available.

Up to 1973 the Canadian tar sand operations produced little if any profits. Balance sheets showed lots of red ink! The increased prices for crude oil following the 1973 oil embargo produced profits from the tar sands for the first time.

Tar sand deposits in the U.S. are not as rich as those in Canada. They will require even higher crude prices to be economic.

Nuclear Fuels

Nuclear fuels have entered the competitive energy market through power generation. They should supply an increasing share of future energy for generation of electricity even though present installations appear marginally economic. Political, ecological and economical problems beset immediate expansion in nuclear fuel use. Calefaction of rivers, disposal of waste products, and public concern over radioactive material have contributed to a reduction in the pace of construction of nuclear-fueled plants. Nevertheless, this fuel will become increasingly important. The tremendous energy requirements of the future will cause all fuel sources to expand.

Coal

We must never forget that both gasoline and natural gas can be manufactured from coal. Thus, the price of this conversion affects the ceiling on future oil and gas prices.

As in the case of nuclear fuels, the future of coal expansion is related to more than economic factors. Air quality requirements, wildcat strikes of coal miners, restrictions relating to strip mining and land withdrawal will affect the quantity of future supplies. The longest strike of coal miners in U.S. history ended in 1978. In shifting the major emphasis in energy resources to coal, significant problems in supply could occur. As indicated by the 1977–1978 coal strike, the problem might be one of continuity of mining, not availability of resource.

End-use Competition

The petroleum industry faces end-use competition which reflects back to basic raw materials. The electric car could affect the oil industry since there are several alternate fuels for generating electricity.

Interfuel competition will limit the price charged for any one fuel source. The ceiling will be the price of the most reasonable alternate fuel.

The Trend Toward More Hostile Environments

One of the dramatic changes in the petroleum industry during the past decade has been the discovery of hydrocarbons in very hostile environments. These environments exist from the Arctic climate of northern Alaska to water depths of 1,000 ft or greater in the ocean off California. The effect of these environments is to magnify risk and to increase costs; and these two factors mean that economic analyses are vital to proper managerial choices. In the inland United States, the trend toward greater drilling depths produces similar requirements.

The Effect of Depth

Depth alone produces significant changes. For example:

- Higher drilling costs
- Costs increase exponentially with depth even for a normal troublefree well. With depth, however, come increasing chances for mechanical problems, all of which add to cost.
- Well density is less at depth. This factor reduces available information about potential reservoirs. Thus, risks increase with the uncertainties regarding reservoir quality.

The trend toward greater producing depths is apparent from the data plotted on Fig. 1–1. Each point reflects a new depth record for production. Although there were significant changes in depth of production in 1938 and 1956, the trend toward deeper production has been almost linear for the past 40 years. One need only extrapolate this trend to estimate possible future producing depths. To date, the

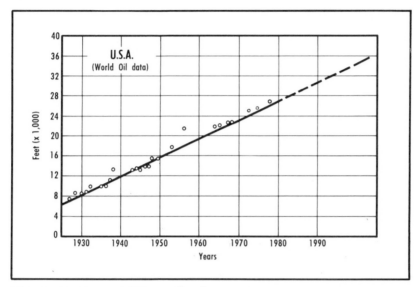

Fig. 1-1   Deepest U.S. productive pay

depth limitation has been drilling technology, not lagging interest in deep prospects on the part of the geologist.

Cost Increases not Associated with Depth

Significant cost increases not associated with depth are also occurring. For example, geophysical costs are increasing. Crew costs have increased because of complex shooting patterns, common-depth-point procedures, increasing material and personnel costs, and increases in the right-of-way (permit) costs. The computer processing of digital seismic data is another factor of higher cost.

Increases in acreage costs have occurred in the past decade. An increasing proportion of lease bonuses involves sealed bid sales. These sales place the bidder at the disadvantage of knowing only his own bid—in contrast to the auction bid or negotiated price under competition. They produce greater revenue for the seller but represent a higher cost to the buyer. We would not be concerned about higher bonus costs if profitable bids were assured. Such is not the case, however. In a sealed bid sale, the arithmetic mean of all bids on a single tract probably represents a profitable estimate of pre-drilling value (which may have little relationship to postdrilling value).

Because the highest bid always succeeds, the odds favor an overall marginal profit.[1][2]

Other acreage costs are also changing. Higher rental payments, shorter lease terms and higher royalty requirements all add to costs.

Governmental Controls

A third element in cost increases involves regulation, particularly Federal regulation. Government regulation covers such important areas as lease sales, pollution control, pipeline approval (safety and right-of-way) and price regulation (or influence).

The first edition of *Exploration Economics* recognized the impending changes in industry-government relations. In the ensuing years the pace of change has been more rapid than anticipated. In fact most of the changes affecting the petroleum industry since 1970 have been political, regulatory or legislative in nature.

The following paragraphs briefly describe the significant changes since 1970. Both beneficial and adverse changes have taken place. The beneficial changes will be reviewed first.

The Beneficial Changes

1. *Price*. One of the beneficial changes has been increases in the wellhead price for both crude oil and natural gas.

The highest prices in the history of the petroleum industry were reached in the early 1980s. In addition, crude oil prices were decontrolled and portions of the controls on natural gas expired. A futures market now exists for crude oil with buyers bidding for tomorrow's supplies as well as hedging against expected price changes. Even a portion of the available natural gas supplies is moving toward a market-oriented price situation.

Although prices have dropped substantially below their peaks in the early 1980s, prices in the mid-1980s were still (on a common dollar base) higher than throughout most of the history of the petroleum industry.

As a consequence of price changes, exploratory and development activities in the early 1980s reached the highest levels in the history of the petroleum industry. The peaks in activity affected all aspects of petroleum exploration—exploratory wells, seismic crew months, acreage acquisitions, employment of technical and nontechnical personnel, etc. The industry amply demonstrated a direct response to price increases.

In the mid-1980s it was a different story. Demand was down, supplies of crude oil and natural gas then were abundant and prices were falling. Again, as a response to price (in this case a lowering of price), activity was down and declining. However, prices in the mid-1980s can still produce profitable results for the more carefully selected exploratory plays.

Natural gas has been a special case. Until 1978 the intrastate market escaped price controls. It provided an interesting comparison to the controlled market of interstate natural gas. Supplies for the interstate market slowly tightened as price controls reduced supplies. Meanwhile, the intrastate prices increased in the unregulated market. Producers of natural gas sought an intrastate market whenever possible. The Natural Gas Policy Act of 1978 (NGPA) changed conditions substantially. It brought intrastate prices for natural gas under Federal price controls. Numerous categories of natural gas were assigned different conditions of price control. The only beneficial feature of the NGPA was the complete deregulation of deep gas (from wells drilled deeper than 15,000 feet). For the deregulated gas, the result was a sharp stimulation in the search for new and deeper natural gas supplies.

Eroding prices for crude oil by the mid-1980s, abrogation of take-or-pay contracts for natural gas, and the expiration of NGPA controls on some categories of natural gas have lowered the demand for high cost gas. Again, one of the causes was interfuel competition and competition of one natural gas supply with another.

In general, price changes since 1970 have been beneficial to the petroleum industry. Historic relationships indicate that the prices of the early 1980s were unusual. The normal price for crude oil (on a common dollar base) has been around $10 per barrel—for the last 50 years.

2. *Prorationing is gone.* This change is beneficial in that the near capacity production of state allowables has shortened payouts and thus increased cash flow. Well allowables, based on spacing and depth, still exist—so do determinations of MER (maximum efficient rate) for reservoirs. However, since the early 1970s the oil and gas fields of the U.S. have been producing at capacity. There are still "take or pay" conditions in contracts for natural gas, but in most instances these terms apply to few fields today.

3. *Corporate income tax is lowered.* In 1978 the Federal tax rate on corporate income was reduced from 48% to 46%. This slight reduction did not influence exploratory decisions, but it did free modestly more cash for reinvestment by the petroleum industry. In

1987 the corporate tax rate was reduced further to 34%. The tax reductions were one of the favorable changes.

4. *Crude oil price deregulation* in 1981 has been a boon to the petroleum industry. It sharply stimulated oil exploration and infill drilling (drilling more wells in existing fields) in older reservoirs. Under price controls, it was not profitable to drill more wells in the old fields as they had the most harsh control of prices. The result of deregulation and the higher prices of the early 1980s was a surprising ability of the U.S. petroleum industry to maintain its producing level around 8.5 million barrels per day—in a period of declining reserve additions from new oil discoveries.

The positive result from these changes is the industry's ability to produce small discoveries previously considered uneconomic.

The Adverse Changes

Many of the significant changes will ultimately stifle the increased activity. They represent the adverse changes since 1970.

1. *The most significant negative change has been in persuasive regulation,* particularly at the Federal level. In 1970 the environmental impact statement (EIS) had not been born nor had many agencies which now regulate oil and gas exploration. Furthermore, the number of agencies contributing to additional paperwork and delay grow more numerous every day. Anyone in the petroleum industry will recognize acronyms of the new entities—DOE, NEPA, OSHA, NOIAA, FERC, ERA and many more. Few congressional legislators knew of the complexities of the petroleum industry. Few still do today. As a result poorly written laws, vague and ambiguous, produced numerous illogical rulings which represent compromises of conflicting views. The prime example of illogical regulatory rulings was the "entitlements" concept promulgated by FEA. In effect successful explorers have to pay others to use their own crude oil—which was regulated at an arbitrarily low price. Consequences of years of price control for interstate sales of natural gas produced no insight for legislators. The simplest laws of economics show that price regulation produces scarcity, not abundance.

Of course, the recipients of entitlements, the small refiners and east coast refiners, do not see them as onerous. One man's penalty given to another is a welcome bounty.

The end result of the new regulation for industry is overlapping duplicity and mountains of paperwork. Massaging paper neither finds nor develops new energy sources.

2. *Changes in tax laws have also occurred.* Percentage depletion is gone for new discoveries for all but the smallest companies. Furthermore, even the depletion for small operators was phased downward—to 15% in 1984. The effect of the loss reduces the industry's cash flow.

3. *Inflation* bounced around considerably in the 1970s. The rate of inflation reached 11% in 1974, but peaked again in the 1979–1982 period at 14%; it subsided by the late 1980s to a level (three to four percent per year) somewhat akin to that of the 1960s.

In periods of high inflation, profits seem unusually high because today's profits come from yesterday's discoveries—already paid for. Inflation robs future profits by mortgaging future discoveries, in effect saddling them with large front-end expenditures which may not be recovered. Some leases purchased in the Outer Continental Shelf (OCS) in the 1980–82 boom will never pay back the large bonuses paid on expectations of future price inflation.

Uncertainty is the one word which described the changes which have occurred since 1970. Government policy represents a new and fluctuating and unpredictable variable. One rule, regulation or stroke of a pen can wipe out a forecast or unhinge all evaluations.

So, there have been good changes and bad changes. Activity has been up and down in the 1980s and recovery from the levels of the mid-1980s seems destined to take some time—a matter of years. The positive mostly outweighed the negative, but the uncertainty produced by over-regulation, inflation and changing tax laws looms ever larger as a limiting factor to the growth in new energy supplies.

Whatever their view about the changes, most thought leaders in the U.S. now fully comprehend the vital role that energy plays in the national well-being—indeed to life itself!

The skillful selection of investments necessitates an understanding of all factors inhibiting profits. Government regulation is one of the most difficult factors to predict. Yet its influence increases every year. The petroleum analyst must weigh all factors affecting a proposed recommendation. Even though many of these factors are beyond his control, the explorationist nevertheless must consider them and be cognizant of their significance to his proposals. Exploration economics must include more than just exploratory costs.

REVIEW

1. The future of any business depends upon the proper selections from possible investments.
2. Increasing costs in all segments of exploration, deeper drilling depths, new hostile operating environments and more intensive state and Federal regulation mean that economics is in your future.

BIBLIOGRAPHY

1. Capen, E.C., Clapp, R.V., and Campbell, W.M., "Competitive Bidding in High Risk Situations," paper given at 45th Annual Fall Meeting of SPE of AIME, October 1970.
2. Megill, R.E., *An Introduction To Risk Analysis, 2 ed.*, PennWell Publishing Co., Tulsa, Oklahoma, 1984, p. 171.

2 Regulation—A Dynamic Force

The petroleum industry was essentially an unregulated industry until the 1930s. The discovery of East Texas field in 1930 caused an oversupply problem of unprecedented magnitude. To prevent utter chaos in a vital industry and to prevent physical waste of a natural resource, the various state governments established regulatory agencies.

At first, their principal task was to prevent the waste of hydrocarbons and to ensure each producer a pro rata share of production. As the industry evolved into a more mature segment of business, other considerations ensued. For a thorough review of state conservation read "A Study of Conservation of Oil & Gas in the United States" published by the Interstate Oil Compact Commission.

In 1970 the U.S. was trending toward capacity production in oil and natural gas. The nation's production of both oil and natural gas peaked in the early 1970s. As of 1978 the petroleum industry in the U.S. was producing crude oil essentially at capacity and was near capacity for production of natural gas. As capacity production continued, imports or alternate energy sources (coal, nuclear fuels, etc.) had to fill the energy gap.

One might think with no surplus capacity existing that regulation would diminish. Quite the opposite occurred. Regulation of the oil and gas industry intensified and became even more of an economic factor. Regulation of various kinds will always be with us; thus, a general review of its significance follows.

The chaos in a vital industry and the loss and waste of the states' resources (and thereby revenue) focused attention on the need for control.

Thus, crude oil proration was born. Proration is the restriction of production based on the market needs of purchasers of oil and gas.

13

To administer proration it was necessary to have regulatory bodies. To the oil producing states, that first answered the need for control, fell the design of regulatory agencies.

State Agencies

In most states regulation is primarily the function of a single agency. These agencies stemmed from conservation laws passed by state legislatures.

Their task was to determine the immediate problems and to devise adequate regulations for the proper administration of conservation statutes. The names of the dominant regulatory bodies for several states are listed below:

Alaska	Dept. of Natural Resources
Oklahoma & Kansas	Corporation Commission
New Mexico	Oil Conservation Division
California	Department of Oil & Gas
Louisiana	Louisiana Oil Conservation Commission
Texas	Railroad Commission

Regulation in Texas

Because Texas is such an important oil producer, a brief discussion of regulatory activity in that state follows.

A review of regulation in Texas will not be absolutely typical of regulation in other states; nevertheless, something of the broad aspects of regulation, conservation and proration common to all producing states can be learned by reviewing a single state. In addition Texas is a producer of sizable quantities of both oil and gas; as such its regulatory bodies have faced most of the problems of conservation.

In Texas, the Railroad Commission (RRC) supervises the regulation of the oil and gas industry. A few activities, involving state land, are regulated by the General Land Office. This body determines the timing and extent of state lease sales. It must approve unitization of pooling agreements involving state lands.

Another state agency, the Texas Department of Water Resources, regulates the industry with regard to the protection of fresh-water sands. This agency approves cementing and casing programs for wells to be drilled including those drilled to dispose of salt water. However, in general, the Texas Railroad Commission has the primary responsibility for regulating most aspects of the oil and gas industry.

The Railroad Commission is composed of three commissioners elected at large. Current commissioners recognize economic as well as physical waste. It was not always so. Texas' oil and gas conservation policies were created out of the necessity to stop wasteful practices rampant in the industry. Current policies have evolved with the increasing knowledge about reservoir behavior, political pressure, changing economic conditions, supply and demand considerations, court rulings, changing technology, changing environmental concepts, and a maturing industry. Present policies are a curious mixture of logic, tradition and rules of thumb.

What does the Railroad Commission regulate? Its responsibilities cover many aspects of the petroleum industry. The chief responsibilities of the commission are as follows:

1. To regulate the quantity of oil or gas flowing from a tract.
2. To determine well spacing.
3. To authorize or force pooling of acreage (interests) for conservation purposes.
4. To exercise pollution control over production and transportation activities by establishing adequate safeguards.
5. To set conservation standards for and to regulate additional recovery projects.
6. To formulate proration policies.

Common Terms

A small but special vocabulary relates to the regulation of oil and gas fields. Some terms are common to both oil and gas fields while others are not. The following terms apply to both oil and gas fields:

1. *Field (common terminology).* The general area underlain by one or more reservoirs formed by a common structural or stratigraphic feature is commonly called an oil or gas field. *Example:* Alazan, North field.
2. *Field (RRC designation).* The RRC uses the above field definition when referring to *all* the reservoirs in a field area, but *also* uses the term to refer to a *single* reservoir (commonly called RRC field): *Example:* Alazan, North (H-21 Sand) field.
3. *Well spacing.* Spacing rules regulate the number and location of wells completed in the *same reservoir.*

The regulations are normally stated as minimum permissible distances from lease lines and between wells. They essentially force each well to drain a specific number of productive acres (proration unit) within the operator's own lease. *Example:* 467'-1200' well spacing (which means 467' minimum from the lease line and 1200' between wells) results in 40-acre proration units.

4. *Proration unit.* The proration unit regulates the number of wells completed in the same reservoir (RRC field).

   The regulations usually state the number of acres which must be assigned to each well. This rule establishes a pattern of well density for adequate drainage of the reservoir and thereby eliminates the drilling of unnecessary wells.

5. *Allowable allocation formulae* are methods for dividing the total allowable production of an oil or gas reservoir among the operators of the various leases in a manner *considered equitable* by the RRC. *Examples:* Allocation formulae are based 100% on productive acreage (*most common*), on number of wells, one-third well—two-thirds acreage, acre-ft and so forth.

6. *Field rules* are those set forth by the RRC to ensure orderly development and exploitation in a specific field. They may apply to *one, several* or all RRC fields (reservoirs) in a general area. They usually include spacing rules, density rules (proration units) and an allowable allocation formula—but may include special or unique provisions such as a gas-oil ratio limit or casing requirements. Field rules are normally requested by one or more operators in an open hearing before the Railroad Commission.

7. *Statewide rules* are a set of general rules applied to all fields (reservoirs) unless specifically amended by field rules. Certain statewide rules apply to all fields, including those with field rules. An example is Rule 37 which is the statewide spacing rule.

8. *Exception to statewide Rule 37.* This rule allows flexibility in locating wells in conflict with existing spacing rules.

Terms Relating to Oil Proration

Additional terms relate specifically to oil wells and the production prorated to each well. The symbols or letters in parentheses are those used in RRC publications on allowables. The terms are:

1. Top zone allowable (TZA) is the maximum per well allowable granted to completions in a specific reservoir. It is most often based on depth yardsticks, but with many exceptions.
2. Depth yardsticks are allowables established by the RRC for statewide application to oil completions. They increase with depth and spacing. See Appendix A, Table 1, for a summary of allowables by depth yardsticks.
   a. 1947 yardsticks apply to RRC fields (reservoirs) discovered prior to 1965.
   b. 1965 yardsticks include greater incentives for deeper drilling and wider spacing. They apply to RRC fields discovered since 1965. Since, by definition, a reservoir is a RRC field, 1965 yardsticks apply to new reservoirs in old fields.
3. Penalized allowables instead of a TZA. Some wells have penalized allowables. Two such allowables are:
   a. High gas-oil ratio (*). Well production is penalized for casinghead gas production in excess of gas-oil ratio limits to conserve reservoir energy. The daily gas limit for each well is determined by multiplying the TZA by the penalty GOR (usually 2,000 cubic feet per barrel).
   b. Limited capacity (#). This is an allowable fixed below TZA because of inability to demonstrate productive capacity.
4. A scheduled allowable is the top zone or penalized allowable of a well as it appears on the RRC schedule.
5. A proration factor (or market demand factor) is the percentage of its scheduled allowable that a well is permitted to produce on a calendar-day basis. Since April 1972, this factor has been 100% for all fields. The Railroad Commission can reduce the factor in a field to prevent waste or for the entire state if demand for crude oil is lower than supply.
6. Exempt allowables are not subject to market variation. (In the case of an exempt allowable, the scheduled allowable is the same as the calendar-day allowable.)
   a. A discovery allowable (NPX) is a higher allowable than the standard depth yardstick. The NPX allowable is assigned to onshore wells in a new field until the eleventh well is drilled or for 24 months, whichever occurs first.
   b. A marginal allowable (M) is used to prevent premature abandonment of economically marginal wells.
   c. Other (X) allowables may be granted for various reasons.

Terms Relating to Gas Proration

Gas production is also regulated by state agencies. State regulation of gas wells concerns the production from the well, well spacing, conservation, pollution control and safety.

Oil well allowables are related to a depth and acreage yardstick. Gas well allowables are initially related to the absolute open flow potential. Later, they are related to market demand for gas from each field.

In Texas some of the special terms associated with gas well allowables are listed below:

1. *The absolute open flow potential* (AOFP) is a theoretical value. It is the rate at which a well could flow at the sand face at zero pounds of pressure. The AOFP is a function of reservoir pressure, the product of permeability times thickness (kh), the degree of formation damage and other physical factors.

   Statewide rules require that the AOFP be determined at initial completion of the well and adjusted periodically as the reservoir pressure declines.

2. *Nonassociated gas well allowables:*
   a. For fields without field rules, Statewide Rule 29 fixes the allowable at 25% of the AOFP. Exceptions can be obtained in late stages of depletion to prevent waste or loss of production. An example would be a well loading up with water when produced at a low rate.
   b. *Field rules.* Where field rules exist, the total field allowable is determined from the demand for gas from the field. The total field allowable, as determined, is divided among the wells based on the allocation formula.

   Special allowables to provide flexibility have been granted in fields having a single operator and a single royalty interest—providing a demand exists for additional gas. Multiple pay zones may or may not require development as separate fields. (Rulings in this area can significantly affect deep drilling economics.)

3. *Associated gas well allowables:*
   a. Statewide Rule 49(B) covers allowables for wells in the gas cap of a reservoir. The gas allowable is set equal to the daily gas limit of an oil well plus the reservoir volume equivalent to the same well's oil allowable.

    b. Sometimes associated gas reservoirs get special allowables as the oil column nears depletion.

    4. Natural gas liquid production (lease condensate and plant liquids) is a function of gas production, and normally limited only by gas allowable, except in a few gas cycling projects. In these projects, permission is usually requested to cycle at a specific rate or to limit liquid production to some maximum volume.

The average explorationist will not need to become familiar with these terms. In most evaluations you should consult the local reservoir engineering group (or production geologists) before setting up a schedule of production from a well or field. These two groups understand the terms and their use and give assistance in this area. The terms are provided and defined as a reference. A limited knowledge of the terms is of value, however. Terms related to regulation vary somewhat from state to state. See *Handbook for the Oil & Gas Industry* (available at Southern Microfilm Reports, Inc., Metairie, Louisiana) for terms used in Louisiana. For Oklahoma, read *Regulations of the Oklahoma Corporation Commission,* Conservation Division.

At the start of every economic evaluation (whether of a prospect, play, or basin), one of the first steps involves a scheduling of production. One must learn therefore what well allowables are applicable to the investment or prospect being evaluated.

Federal Regulation

As we noted, states bore the initial burdens of regulation. Their interest was conservation of a wasting asset for the benefit of their citizens and for the protection of individual property rights. Within the past three decades, Federal regulation has become increasingly important. It affects both oil and gas production.

If someone in the year 1970 could have predicted the degree of increased Federal regulation that existed in the 1980s, his forecast would have been rejected. No one at that time foresaw the almost unbelievable magnitude of Federal regulation which would have come from the halls of Congress. The National Environmental Policy Act had been passed in 1969. The Clean Air Act followed in 1970. These new Acts placed unprecedented power in the hands of regulatory agencies. The full impact of these laws has just begun to reach affected industries. Furthermore, these two Acts were but harbingers of others to follow. Examples are:

Federal Water Pollution Control Act—1972
Coastal Zone Management Act—1972
Coastal Zone Management Act (Amendments)—1976
Endangered Species Act—1973
Federal Land Policy Management Act—1976

The avalanche of legislation has not slowed. Bills pending before Congress would increase the scope of regulation. Little by little the exploration of mineral resources and the multiple use concept of land are being choked to the point of inhibiting development. Yet our need and consumption of resources continue to increase.

The Department of Energy

In 1977 the Department of Energy (DOE) was formed. Its formation was instituted to consolidate under one department several agencies dealing with energy policy, resource development, land usage, etc. At the same time, the Federal Power Commission (which controlled and regulated interstate gas pipelines and interstate gas prices) was renamed the Federal Energy Regulatory Commission (FERC). The commission has an ill-defined relationship to portions of the DOE, but mostly to the Economic Regulatory Administration, a unit of DOE. FERC is not, however, responsible to the Secretary of the Department of Energy. It is an independent body in the regulatory arena of Washington.

The Effect

Many claims have surfaced regarding the benefits of these new agencies, regulatory bodies and departments. No matter what the claims, two results stand self-evident—delay and paperwork.

Of course, delay to a nonprofit organization has little meaning. To business and industry it means loss—loss of money and opportunity. Added delays and redundant paperwork mean tying up people and assets in activities which produce no new product, no new service and no revenue.

The evidence of the effect on industry (not just the petroleum industry) of new and often overlapping regulations is just beginning to appear. It is unfortunate that the small operator will be most affected.

Regulations are issued in such volume that separate staffs in most companies do little else but monitor new rules and disseminate their effect and requirements to operating groups. The company too small for such a staff can easily find itself violating the law—unaware of the law's existence.

What Does it all Mean?

Life for the explorationist has become much more complex. Any projection of future development, prices, inflation, production, and facility installation must now take into account increasing numbers of rules. Furthermore, such rules and regulations are ever expanding. So, in evaluating an investment opportunity, the analyst must be much more versed in existing and pending law than ever before.

Does your offshore location require an archeological survey? Do you have baseline studies completed for ambient air requirements to secure a permit for a gas plant? Has your rig been permitted to drill in this or that ocean area? Have you filed a working plan for exploratory development on Federal lands? Such are the questions which can impact your estimate of development rate for a new prospect.

In practice the analyst must locate within his own organization those persons knowledgeable about each regulatory area. In a major company, the Natural Gas Department will have knowledge about existing wellhead prices and possible pending legislation affecting future prices. The Production Department (or Drilling Department) will know of existing rig or location limitations for your prospects. Some companies have in each department a small environmental affairs group. This group sifts from the voluminous Federal Register the new laws, rules or regulations affecting their function. In the absence of such a group, check your Legal Department or law representative.

The Special Case of Natural Gas

Sales of natural gas in the interstate market have endured the longest regulatory history for the petroleum industry. The Federal Energy Regulatory Commission (formerly the Federal Power Commission) has specific regulatory responsibilities involving natural gas moving in interstate commerce. Interstate transportation and sale of natural gas are regulated for protection of consumers. Such regulation involves fixing wellhead prices for natural gas. Prices are fixed by broad areas:

inland nationwide
Outer Continental Shelf
possibly the North Slope of Alaska

Historically, prices for interstate gas have been restrictive. The result was rapid growth in supplies for the previously unregulated intrastate market and diminished supplies for the interstate market. New discoveries sought the intrastate market where possible. Contracts there were still negotiated at arms length and little regulation or paperwork was involved. The inertia of regulation plagues the FERC, reducing its ability to keep pace with rapidly changing conditions and it will be increasingly difficult for it to do so. In 1978 legislation passed by Congress extended price control by FERC to intrastate sales of natural gas. The history regarding interstate gas supplies does not show this change to be any solution to funding new supplies of natural gas. In the long run, the answer may well depend on importation of liquefied natural gas (LNG) or synthetic natural gas (SNG) derived from coal or shale. Both sources would produce gas at much higher prices.

Natural gas from Alaska and possibly Mexico will supplement imports from Canada. Imports of natural gas fall under FERC control.

Changes at DOI

The Department of the Interior (DOI) exists as a separate body from other regulatory agencies, although it must now coordinate its efforts with the Department of Energy (DOE). In the early 1980s the DOI set up a new division to handle offshore leasing, previously handled by the Bureau of Land Management (BLM). The new division was named the Minerals Management Service (MMS). In one sense, the new division was created to answer questions from a Congress perennially concerned with the question "Is the U.S. government getting fair market value for its leases in the Outer Continental Shelf?"

The Minerals Management Service was initially formed from pieces of the BLM and the Conservation Division of DOI. In some instances (offshore lease bidding methods for example) the proposals of DOI are subject to DOE review. Nevertheless, the Department of the Interior, through the MMS, determines the timing and extent of Federal offshore lease sales.

Federal lands, however, involve onshore as well as offshore. Offshore tracts in Federal waters are leased through sealed bid sales and some onshore tracts also (on known geologic structures). However, part of the Federal land, particularly in the Rocky Mountain states, can be leased for a nominal filing fee. Such tracts are awarded by lottery. Onshore, the BLM manages the mineral rights for Federal lands and the Forest Service handles the surface rights.

Texas and Louisiana regulatory bodies initially regulated production per well in the Gulf of Mexico. Now the DOI (through the MMS) has assumed regulatory authority over production from offshore leases in the Gulf of Mexico. It and other departments probably will assume more and more regulatory authority in the decades ahead.

Gas Contracts

As long as gas supply was abundant, gas contracts were reasonably uniform. Guaranteed takes were spaced over a number of years to ensure a steady, adequate supply for the pipeline purchaser. The normal contract had such general terms as:

1. A negotiated magnitude of the total reserve contracted.
2. A daily contract quantity (DCQ) usually 1 $\overline{M}$ cfd for each 8 billion cu ft of reserve. The DCQ is usually referred to as the "take."
3. A contracted price. If interstate, it was set by FERC. If intrastate, it was a negotiated price. The contract price is often related to gas quality (BTU content).
4. In intrastate contracts, some form of price escalation.
5. A committed area (sometimes with a depth limitation) assigned to the contract which may include new reservoirs or extensions to existing reservoirs.
6. Provisions for reserve redetermination. Such provisions allow for an adjustment of the take.

Temporary conditions of supply shortage existed in the late 1970s. Cold winters usually point out distribution as well as supply inadequacies and the colder-than-normal winters of the late 1970s did just that. The short-term condition of shortage rapidly changed to what was called the gas "bubble," a condition of surplus. In fact, throughout most of the history of the natural gas industry, there has been a gas bubble. The "one-to-eight" contract was a recognition of a bubble.

The pre-bubble conditions (1978–1980) spawned new contract conditions, some of which were later abrogated in the bubble era to follow. The new conditions included faster takes, higher prices, investment prepayments (on the part of the purchaser), early price renegotiation and faster price escalation.

In just a short time, consumption of natural gas decreased (related to higher prices and interfuel competition) and producers of natural gas were stunned to find purchasers abrogating contract agreements. Such abrogation had seldom if ever occurred before. The bubble era of 1983–1987 was almost an about-face of the short undersupply conditions. A spot market developed for natural gas supplies as producers sought markets for new discoveries. Takes (production purchases) were reduced and negotiations softened "take-or-pay" agreements (those not abrogated).

These rapid changes in just a decade (from surplus to shortage to surplus) once again depict the strong interfuel competition that always exists if the market is not over-regulated. Gas contract provisions are vital inputs in any economic evaluation. The analyst must understand contract provisions to employ them in his calculations of prospect or play economics. For this reason, it is wise to keep up to date on the latest trends in contract provisions; or at least consult with a market specialist on expected terms for sale of gas from a potentially productive new play.

Other Regulatory Influences

Other forces tend to act as regulatory influences. Some of these forces are:

1. The President of the United States and the economic advisors of the Executive Branch of the Federal government.
2. State and Federal legislatures.
3. City and county governments. Any drilling within a city will necessitate a review of the city's restrictions. County governments have restrictions relating to heavy loads on local roads.
4. Joint interest owners.
5. Royalty owners.
6. Competitors. Occasionally, a competitor will initiate an action out of pattern to normal practice. It may set the pattern for future action. It may also influence future legislation if the practice is of questionable legality.
7. Public opinion (which can be a strong regulator).
8. Supply-demand expectations. What a company expects to happen to total U.S. (world) supply-demand conditions can affect its operations.

With dwindling oil reserves prorationing ended, but regulation did not. The nation's regulatory bodies find themselves regulating more and more over less and less.

In Figure 2–1, the ratio of reserves to production for the U.S. is plotted from 1960 to 1985. Gas reserves at Prudhoe (26 tcf) are not being produced. This factor and lower gas consumption (interfuel competition) have flattened the downward trend in the ratio for natural gas. The decline has been from a ratio of reserves to production of 20 tcf in 1960, to the 11 to 12 level in the mid-1980s.

Before Prudhoe Bay, the ratio of reserves to production for crude oil in the U.S. had reached a low of 9.3 tcf in 1969. Reserves at Prudhoe Bay jumped the ratio back to 12. From that level the trend has been inexorably downward as the industry continues to produce reserves faster than it replaces them. At consumption rates of the 1980s, the U.S. will never again be self-sufficient in crude oil production.

Normally at capacity the ratio of reserves to production nears the range of 6 to 8. We should expect the curves in Fig. 2–1 to approach these levels with gas lagging behind oil until production at Prudhoe Bay starts. Without Prudhoe Bay's reserves of natural gas, the U.S. ratio in 1985 would have been near 10—instead of 12. The value of 10

Fig. 2–1   U.S. ratio of reserves to production (Source: API, AGA, DOE)

means that there is not a lot of excess capacity for natural gas production in the U.S., at least by historic standards.

The Shift in Regulation

In the Carter administration the most significant change in regulation was the subtle shift from regulation in terms of what is lawful, to regulation of how to perform normal business functions. Regulation moved from an advisory to a participatory role. The Reagan administration attempted to diminish the government's role with limited success. The degree and amounts of regulation existing in the late 1980s is far greater than in the pre-Carter administration period. So the industry has had to learn to deal with new forms of government rules, regulations and concerns.

To the explorationist desiring to measure the profitability of a prospect or a play, regulation will be important. It affects future costs and prices. The analyst must determine how, in what way, and by whom his hydrocarbon deposit will be regulated and fit the consequences (cost, well spacing, price, production rate, etc.) into his evaluation. Consideration of regulation is a first step. For this reason it is discussed in the first part of this book.

REVIEW

1. Regulation of oil and gas production was born out of the chaos and waste in a young industry.
2. As the industry has matured, so have regulatory concepts.
3. The U.S. petroleum industry has reached capacity production of its oil and gas reserves.
4. Regulation in the future will continue to emphasize conservation, but there will be even greater emphasis on pollution and environmental control.
5. Because a schedule of production is one of the early steps in the evaluation of an exploration opportunity, a general understanding of regulation is necessary.

3 Understanding the Terms

We have progressed to a point where some useful terms must be defined. Exploration expenditures are budgeted, tabulated, and recorded in various records. In this chapter the accounting terms relating to exploration analysis will be introduced. We shall concern ourselves with the types of records normally kept by a corporation. Those with a more simple recording system can adjust accordingly. The terms introduced are the important aspect, rather than a specific recording method.

We will introduce one term at a time by discussion. The terms and associated expenditures will be followed from first investment to final profits. An exploration budget will be developed and budget categories related to the corporate books—which brings us to our first definition.

> *Corporate books:* The method of accounting used to report financial results to management and stockholders.

The method of accounting illustrated in this chapter is the "successful efforts" method in which (most) unsuccessful efforts or losses are deducted in the year spent.

The Birth of an Idea—We Isolate a Lead

Explorationists are familiar with Wallace Pratt's phrase, "oil is found in the minds of men."

Ideas generated by geologists and geophysicists start the investment chain which ultimately leads to the discovery of hydrocarbons. In terms of an exploration budget, idea generation expenditures are represented by the salaries of technical people and have the budget classification of geological and geophysical costs. Salaries and other office expenditures (rent, telephone, supplies, etc.) are usually expensed on accounting records.

Definitions: Expenditures deducted from income in the year of expenditure are said to be *expensed.* Expenditures deducted from income over the years of useful life of an asset are said to be *capitalized.* Equipment expenditures are usually capitalized. Capital items often have potential salvage value.

In this chapter for each new term the relationship between its budget category and how the term is handled on a corporation's books will be noted. Table 3–1 shows the budget category, what it is composed of and whether it is expensed or capitalized. This format will be followed for subsequent budget categories.

TABLE 3–1

Exploration Expenditures

Budget category	How handled	
	Capitalized	Expensed
Geological		Salaries, rent, telephone, etc.
Geophysical		Salaries, supplies, contract services
Management (Overhead and other)		Salaries, supplies, contract services, allocated costs
General plant	Geological warehouse, laboratory equipment; geophysical equipment; office equipment	

Following Up the Idea—A Prospect Emerges

Once an idea emerges, its follow-up begins. Additional subsurface maps are drawn and seismic crews set to work. Acreage purchases may ensue. These purchases will involve subsequent rental payments and taxes on unoperated acreage. The terms involved in these activities are defined and the proper budget categories noted in Table 3–2.

Definitions: A cash payment made to acquire a lease on a property is called a *lease bonus.* A company or individual buying

TABLE 3–2

Exploration Expenditures

Budget category	How handled	
	Capitalized	Expensed
Geophysical crews		Salaries, supplies, contract services
Transportation equipment	Seismic crews, trucks and autos	
General Plant	Seismic crews, digital equipment	
Land		Salaries, supplies, rent, etc.
Unoperated lease purchases	Lease bonus	
Rentals and taxes		Rentals and taxes on unoperated acreage
Geological core tests		Core drilling costs

the lease is called *lessee*. The person granting the lease is called the *lessor*. Since the bonus represents the buyer's investment in the property, it must be capitalized. The acquisition costs associated with a lease bonus are also capitalized. These costs include:

> abstracts of title
> recording fees and court costs
> certified copies of instruments
> attorney's fees
> title curative-work
> payments to lease brokers

An annual sum paid during the lease life in lieu of development of the property is called a *lease rental*. Lease rentals are expensed.

Lease bonus is one of the few capitalized budget items which has no salvage value (unless sold to another party before cancellation).

Testing the Idea—We Get a Discovery

Assuming that geological and geophysical investigations confirm the original idea, a prospect is born. The prospect can now be tested by several means:

1. A wildcat well can be drilled.
2. A farmout or trade can be made retaining a working interest.
3. A test well contribution can be made to promote an exploratory well.

TABLE 3–3

Drilling Cost Analysis

Location _____ Rig contractor _____
Lease _____
Well number _____
Depth-proposed _____ Drilled _____ Date completed _____
Classification: Oil _____ Gas _____ Drilling days _____

Intangible costs

	Total	Per day	Per foot
Site costs	___	___	___
Transportation-rig	___	___	___
Rig operations	___	___	___
Drilling fluid	___	___	___
Formation evaluation	___	___	___
Casing cement	___	___	___
Completion tools	___	___	___
Perforating	___	___	___
Squeeze cementing	___	___	___
Formation stimulation	___	___	___
Well supplies	___	___	___
Other	___	___	___
Total intangible costs	___	___	___

Tangible costs

	Size	Amount	Cost
Casing			
-Surface	___	___	___
-Intermediate	___	___	___
-Production	___	___	___
-Tubing	___	___	___
Well equipment	___	___	___
Total tangible costs	___	___	___
Total well cost	___		

For the present, assume that we decide to drill a wildcat well. In estimating costs for the proposed well, a drilling cost analysis is usually compiled. Such an analysis appears in Table 3–3. Note that the total cost is separated into tangible and intangible costs.

The reasons for separating drilling costs into tangible and intangible costs will become apparent in subsequent chapters. For now we need to know that the separation must be made and what items go in each category.

Definitions: *Intangible costs* ordinarily do not have a salvage value. They usually account for about 70% of the total cost of an exploratory well.

Tangible well costs ordinarily have some salvage value and average about 30% of total well costs.

Deeper drilling dry hole costs are drilling costs below the deepest producing zone.

Wildcat wells are recorded under the classification of exploratory drilling and appear on budgets as follows:

TABLE 3-4

Exploration Expenditures

Budget category	How handled	
	Capitalized	Expensed
Exploratory drilling	Successful wells	Dry wells
		Deeper drilling dry hole cost in successful wells

Note that on the corporate books all costs relating to dry holes are expensed and all costs for successful wells are capitalized.

A Discovery Leads to Development

If the exploratory well is dry, the entire net cost is expensed (deducted from income), and the prospect goes back into the file or additional study ensues before a second well is drilled.

If successful, a chain of new investments begins. More wells are needed to develop the field; lease facilities (flow lines, tank batteries, metering equipment, etc.) must be installed, and the operation of a producing property begins.

Successful development wells are capitalized on the corporate books as are development dry holes. In the case of development dry holes, the present handling is a change brought about by the Statement of Financial Accounting Standards No. 19 by the Financial Accounting Standards Board.[1] Prior to January 1, 1978, development dry holes were expensed. Successful development wells usually have about 60% intangible costs.

Lease facilities are capitalized. Operating expenses (direct, overhead and benefits) are expensed.

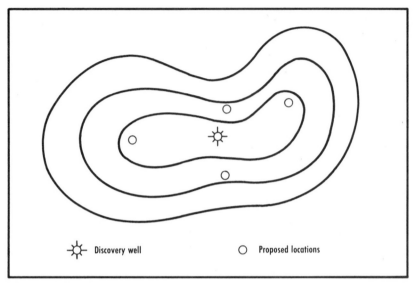

Fig. 3–1   Development following discovery

Definitions: *Direct operating expenses* are costs identified with specific properties or units of production. They include pumper and gang salaries, repair and maintenance of lease facilities, etc.

District overhead is the expense related to operations but which cannot be properly assigned to a specific unit. District overhead is allocated on some rational basis. The term "district" overhead is used to denote the level. It implies operational overhead at the lease level. In major corporations, there are other overhead allocations for larger organizational units (i.e., divisions, headquarters, etc.).

Employee benefit expense includes all benefit expenditures (vacation, sick leave, holidays, etc.).

Operating expenses begin with production and continue until abandonment. Most expenditures after production starts are expensed. However, additional investments still must be capitalized. Examples of these are:

1. Workover for a multiple completion or recompletion in a new reservoir, if successful.
2. Additional lease facilities; e.g., a compressor for a gas lease when wellhead tubing pressure drops below working line pressure.
3. Additional investment for secondary recovery.

Gas plants are a downstream investment subsequent to discovery and are not an exploration investment. These plants are discretionary investments tied to volumes, hydrocarbon composition or special treating needs. Few of these factors are known in a relatively new play; and gas plant economics ordinarily do not greatly affect the yardsticks for judging exploration investments. It is more convenient to assume a plant, if one is needed, and estimate the revenue returning to the leaseholder. After all, you may not build the plant and therefore the plant revenue could go to someone else. For these and other reasons, in this book investment considerations stop at the lease line.

In the event the prospects being evaluated relate to a formation known to carry substantial hydrogen sulfide (H_2S), a plant must be constructed prior to production. In this instance plant investments are calculated and charged to the prospects it serves. The operating expenses for the plant are allocated to the wells served by the plant. These charges usually include a rate of return at or around the minimum acceptable level.

The Successful Prospect Generates Revenue

The consequences of a successful discovery, its development and its operation are a revenue stream. The revenue is generated by the sale of crude oil, condensate, or natural gas from the lease or income credited to the lease from gas plant products (liquids, sulfur, etc.). A company receives its revenue according to its interest in the property.

Definitions: *Revenue* is defined as the money received from the sale of raw material or products.

A *working interest* (W.I.) is a company's portion (%) of total revenue. It also represents the company's obligation toward investment and operating costs.

A *royalty interest* is a retained interest (usually by the landowner or mineral right holder) deducted from a working interest and having no obligation toward investments or operating costs.

A *net interest* is a company's portion of revenue (W.I.) less all royalty interests.

Tax Obligations Arise From Revenue

A profitable producing property creates tax obligations. Out of revenue we pay production, ad valorem, and income taxes. The next chapter is devoted entirely to taxes. They are mentioned here to lead into the calculation of profits from revenue.

How much money does a company keep from the revenue generated by a producing property? What can be deducted from revenue to reduce taxable income legitimately? The items deducted from revenue to reduce taxable income can be divided into two categories—cash and non-cash items. Cash items are those expenditures made during the year and are truly "out-of-pocket" expenses. Non-cash items are deductions allowed from (1) previous expenditures which were capitalized or (2) from depletion. Both types are listed below:

Cash items
1. Direct operating expense
2. District overhead expense
3. Employee benefit costs
4. Production taxes
5. Ad valorem taxes

Non-cash items
1. Depreciation
2. Depletion

Definitions: *Production taxes* are state and municipal taxes levied on oil and gas products, e.g., Texas levies a 4.6% tax on the value of crude oil and condensate and 7.5% on natural gas and natural gas liquids. Production taxes are sometimes called *severance taxes.*

Ad valorem taxes are state or county taxes assessed upon the value of a property.

Depreciation is an annual reduction of income reflecting the loss in useful value of capitalized investments by reason of wear and tear.

Depletion is a reduction in income reflecting the exhaustion of a mineral deposit. It is allowed to prevent the taxation of a capital asset as ordinary income. The following chapter will illustrate the calculation of depletion.

These various deductions are shown in Table 3–5. Cash and non-cash items are deducted directly from revenue to calculate taxable income—the amount of money upon which income taxes must be paid.

Table 3–5 illustrates deductions at the producing lease level. From the total net revenue of all leases, the expenses of higher

TABLE 3–5

**Calculating Taxable Income
at the District Level**

			M$
Revenue			40,000
Less expense items			
Cash items			
Direct operating expense	3,000		
District overhead expense	1,500		
Employee benefit expense	1,000		
Production and ad valorem taxes	4,000		
Total cash items		9,500	
Non-cash items			
Depreciation	5,000		
Depletion	8,800		
Total non-cash items		13,800	
Total expensed items			23,300
Net taxable income			16,700

corporate levels are deducted. Exploration management expenses, research, administrative services, and other allocated costs are examples of such deductions.

A Budget System

We have now followed the generation of a prospect from its inception through development.

How each expenditure was handled on the corporate books has been indicated, and the calculation of taxable income illustrated. Although corporate usage is the reference point, the general approach to budgeting should be applicable even if you are self-employed. In the final section of this chapter, we will illustrate an exploration budget.

A budgeting system assigns funds for investment purposes. Capital budgeting is needed for an individual, partnership, or corporation:

1. To plan future expenditures
2. To review the distribution of expenditures by categories, products, geographic areas, geologic trends, etc.

3. To control capital expenditures to make sure that:
- funds are invested wisely
- investments meet company standards
- investments are financially attractive

Some companies budget only capitalized items; others budget all expenditures, including expensed items. If all expenditures in an exploration program are budgeted, the expensed items will dominate. They may account for as much as 70% of the total exploratory budget.

TABLE 3-6

An Exploration Budget

_____ Organizational unit
_____ Year

Thousands of Dollars

Budget category	Proposed budget	Capitalized	Expensed
Exploratory drilling	9,600	2,900	6,700
Lease purchases	4,500	4,500	—
Core tests	300		300
Geophysical crews	3,100		3,100
Rentals and taxes on unoperated acreage	1,200		1,200
Geological expense	1,500		1,500
Geophysical interpretation	1,400		1,400
Land, scouting, EDP*	1,100		1,100
Overhead	2,000		2,000
Equipment**	250	250	
Total budget	24,950	7,650	17,300

* Geological and geophysical data processing.
** Transportation, special geophysical equipment, general plant, etc.

Definition: For accounting purposes the term _investment_ includes only those items which are capitalized.

An exploration budget represents expenditures for many separate programs in various stages of development. Some are in the idea stage, some in the follow-up stage, and others are in the testing stage. In the sample budget shown in Table 3–6, all expenditures are budgeted. It is symbolic and does not relate to any specific company or organizational unit. It provides a brief review of expensed and capitalized items as shown on the corporate books.

The sample budget tabulated above shows about 30% capitalized items and 70% expensed items. The acquisition costs of acreage leased are included in the budget category of lease purchases. Remember, this representation reflects the corporate books. How we treat these same expenditures for tax purposes is the subject of the next chapter.

REVIEW

1. To illustrate how physical events (wells drilled, acres acquired) are translated into budgets, a prospect was followed from inception to successful completion.
2. Along the way new terms were introduced. We should now understand such terms as expense, capitalize, tangible and intangible.
3. In general for basic accounting records, we capitalize things and expense effort.
4. A company budgets to plan future expenditures, to review the various categories of expenditures and to set up the basis for review, control, and follow-up of investments.

BIBLIOGRAPHY

1. Statement of Financial Accounting Standards No. 19, "Federal Accounting and Reporting by Oil and Gas Producing Companies," Federal Accounting Standards Board, Stamford, Conn., December 1977.

4 Rendering Unto Caesar

This chapter is designed to help you understand tax planning. Anyone who searches for hydrocarbons needs an understanding of tax concepts. Whether you are an independent or work for a major company, taxes affect your efforts. If an independent, you probably have a tax consultant and every major oil company has a tax department. Our purpose is not to replace either. It is to increase your awareness of the need for tax planning and to show the effect of taxes on investment evaluation.

The Importance of Tax Planning

Taxes are big business. Find out what your company pays in taxes and you will realize just how big the tax business has become. Tax concepts in this chapter are oriented to the corporation and corporate tax rates are assumed. Non-corporate and other taxpayers with different tax rates can adjust the presentations used accordingly.

There are important areas of exploration activity where proper tax planning can reduce the company's tax liability. No one will become a tax expert from reading this chapter. Yet, all of you will be more aware of potential tax savings and how taxes affect an investment.

The current Federal income tax rate for corporations is 34%. The corporate tax rate was reduced from 46% to 34% by the Tax Reform Act of 1986. For investment purposes you may wish to use 36 or 37% to account for an average state income tax (if you operate in several states) and for franchise (ad valorum) taxes. In this textbook the rate of 34% is used. A tax rate of this magnitude means that a dollar of deductions from income saves a company (with profits from other operations) 34 cents in Federal income taxes.

With such a burden, a taxpayer must know his rights as well as his duties. Legitimate minimization of taxes (tax avoidance) can be as important as lowering production costs or an increase in sales. In fact a deduction for tax purposes may sometimes be worth several times

38

the same amount in additional sales. For these and many reasons, tax planning makes good sense. Tax planning is the legitimate use of all current laws, regulations, and court decisions concerning taxable income. Tax avoidance is good business planning as opposed to tax evasion which is illegal.

Tax interpretations change periodically from either new legislation or court rulings or Internal Revenue Service practice. To keep informed on significant tax changes and how you are affected, you will need to consult a tax expert; or if you work for a company, check regularly with your tax department.

Important Factors in Oil and Gas Taxation

Each industry has its own particular types of expenditures which affect taxable income. Since Federal income tax began, various laws, IRS rulings and court decisions have developed regulations governing taxable income. In the petroleum industry, there are six areas which require comprehension for proper tax planning. These are:

1. Intangible development costs (IDC).
2. Percentage depletion.
3. Timing of deductions.
4. Capitalization of expenditures.
5. Capital gains provisions.
6. Investment tax credit.

Of these six factors, the first four are of importance to the explorationist. Capital gains regulations seldom affect exploration investment decisions. The investment tax credit (ITC) is a direct credit (deduction) from income tax based on a percentage of qualified capitalized investments. It has varied from seven to ten percent in recent years and is subject to frequent change by Congress. Thus, in any text it becomes impossible to give finite comments on an indefinite subject. However, for the explorationist, ITC, like capital gains, seldom influences an investment decision.

There are other tax considerations not considered here. Among these are passive loss limitations, working interest exceptions, disposition of interest and the alternate minimum tax. These tax provisions seldom change an exploratory decision; they may, however, be important for a specific company or for a given investment. Always consult your tax expert to make certain you have included the proper tax provisions.

Intangible Development Costs (IDC)

Intangible development costs are expenditures which ordinarily do not have a salvage value; they must be essential to the drilling and preparation of wells for production of oil and gas. Items making up intangible drilling costs were shown on the drilling cost form, Table 3-3.

For the corporate books, we said that intangible drilling costs (IDC) are capitalized and depreciated over the life of the producing property. However, IDC are normally handled differently for tax purposes. The Internal Revenue Service (IRS) says that for computing taxable income, a company may capitalize or expense (a portion of) the IDC. Only one choice is possible for each company, and it must be made in the year the company first incurs IDC. Most companies made the choice many years ago—to expense as much IDC as the law allows.

The exact amount of the IDC that can be expensed (deducted from income in the year spent) has varied through the years as tax laws have changed.

For many years the petroleum industry was permitted to expense all IDC. Recent tax law changes have reduced the amount of the IDC that can be expensed. The Tax Reform Act of 1986 reduced the amount of IDC that can be expensed (for integrated companies) to 70%. The remaining 30% must be amortized over a five-year period; that is, the amount is deducted from income over five years in equal amounts every year (straight line depreciation).

Intangible development costs are subject to being reduced if a property is sold. This change was made in the Tax Reform Act of 1976. The tax law states they are subject to "recapture" meaning that, under certain conditions, portions of IDC cannot be claimed and must be reported as ordinary income. Because explorationists normally are not involved in the sale of properties this aspect of tax law is mentioned only to document its existence to protect your tax interest fully. See a tax expert if you sell a property.

A tax savings prevents an outflow of cash in the form of income tax. A company with many investment opportunities may have cash requirements which exceed those generated internally. Capitalizing expenditures defers tax savings and increases current income tax. Expensing expenditures, where allowed, reduces taxable income and thus also reduces Federal income tax. Such a reduction in turn leaves more cash immediately available to be reinvested in new revenue-generating opportunities. In addition, a company receives no practical benefits from capitalizing IDC. More comments on this later.

Percentage Depletion

History. Percentage depletion came into being as a consequence of the income tax amendment to the U.S. Constitution in 1913. Prior to this amendment, there was no need to distinguish, for tax purposes, between income and capital. Capital expenditures generate revenue from which dividends, profits, and taxes are paid. If capital is taxed as ordinary income, the amount available for re-investment diminishes; therefore, tax laws distinguish between capital and income so that capital is retained for future investments. Consider a U.S. Savings Bond. When you pay $75 for a bond, your capital is invested. Later you may cash the bond for $100. The interest (income) of $25 is taxed when cashed, but not the original investment (capital) of $75.

An oil discovery presents some difficult problems in determining its value as an asset. Because of several factors, one of them being risk, a discovery is worth several times the investment in the individual lease on which the discovery well is drilled. To tax all revenue as income would sharply reduce funds for re-investment.

Congress attempted to alleviate the plight of the oil producers with the passage of a law on discovery value depletion in 1918. By this law a producer could deduct the fair market value of his property from income to prevent capital loss. Unfortunately, the fair market value of an oil property is not easily determined in the discovery year; and in 1926, Congress attempted to make the regulations more workable by changing the discovery value concept to a percentage figure. Using the percentage relieved the administrative problems associated with the law and from 1926 to 1969 oil operators were allowed to deduct 27.5% of gross income from a property as percentage depletion (with one limitation to be discussed later).

There was nothing magic about the 27.5%. It was a compromise between 25% and 30% worked out by a congressional committee. It bore an approximate relationship to the average discovery value which the courts allowed in the cases from 1918 to 1926. In the 1969 Tax Reform Act, the depletion percentage for oil and gas properties was revised downward to 22%.

The Tax Reduction Act of 1975 is a mockery of its title. It raised the taxes of the petroleum industry substantially by virtually eliminating percentage depletion except under special conditions.

For large petroleum companies percentage depletion was eliminated except for:

a. natural gas whose price was regulated by the Federal Power Commission (FPC) and was sold prior to July 1, 1976;

b. natural gas sold before Feb. 1, 1975, under a fixed price which could not be adjusted upward to offset tax increases from the loss of depletion.

For small, non-integrated producers percentage depletion continued at 22% of gross revenue until 1980. As shown by the following schedule, it decreased to 15% in 1984.

Year	Daily Average Production-bbl*	Percentage Depletion Rate-%
1975	2,000	22
1976	1,800	22
1977	1,600	22
1978	1,400	22
1979	1,200	22
1980	1,000	22
1981	1,000	20
1982	1,000	18
1983	1,000	16
1984 & thereafter	1,000	15

* or natural gas at 6,000 cubic feet per barrel conversion.

The net effect of the Tax Reduction Act of 1975 was to eliminate depletion on oil for large companies and sharply restrict its application on existing gas sales. Percentage depletion for large companies is gone for new discoveries.

Despite the near loss of depletion, it remains a factor, particularly in tax consequences of trades between a large and small company. For this reason the further definition and discussion of percentage depletion and its calculation are retained in this revised edition.

For the layman one of the best references on depletion is a small booklet published by the Mid-Continent Oil & Gas Association. The title is "Percentage Depletion—Economic Progress and National Security." It is recommended reading for those interested in learning more about percentage depletion.

Further definition. Each producing property has a tax deduction called *allowable depletion*. Allowable depletion is the amount in dollars which may be deducted from taxable income in a year. It is the greater of cost depletion or percentage depletion.

a. Cost depletion is based on the capitalized cost of a mineral property. For example, if you buy producing oil reserves at $1 per barrel, you can by law deduct $1 from income each time a barrel is produced; the $1 is your capital investment and the law always allows a return of capital, i.e., you are always entitled to cost depletion.

b. Percentage depletion

The discoverer of an oil or gas field did not buy a producing property. He recovers his capital through percentage depletion which is 15% of gross income—not to exceed 50% of the net income from the property. The 50% limitation is the one mentioned earlier. In effect it limits the oil operator to no more than the capital gains provision allows nonmineral investments.

It is not beyond the realm of reason to foresee the reinstatement of percentage depletion at some future date. Why? The tax history of the petroleum industry around the world has been one of up and down rates. However, when the needs have been great, incentives have been granted by most governments. Thus, the condition of large capital needs and very scarce resources could generate new depletion incentives. Such incentives would be needed for the development of synthetic crude and natural gas resources (shale oil, coal gasification, etc.).

Allowable Depletion—Its Calculation

To see how allowable depletion is calculated, we must investigate both cost depletion and percentage depletion.

Cost depletion may be expressed as $I \times \dfrac{P}{R}$ where:

I = The investment (actually the undepleted cost in a property, i.e., the original cost less previously deducted depletion).

P = Units (bbls or Mcf) of oil, gas or liquids produced during the year.

R = Units of oil or gas estimated to be left in the reservoir plus current year production.

The definition could also be shown as:

$$\text{Cost depletion} = \text{remaining investment} \times \frac{\text{annual production}}{\text{remaining reserve}}$$

Table 4–1 shows a simple calculation of cost depletion.

TABLE 4–1

Cost Depletion

(Cost figures in thousands)

Year	Reserves-MB $\dfrac{R}{MB}$ Added	Reserves-MB Net	$\dfrac{P}{MB}$ Prod.	$\dfrac{P}{R}$ Unit of Dpl'n.	Lease Cost Added	Lease Cost Total	I Undpl'n. Cost	$\dfrac{P}{I \times R}$ Cost Dpl'n.
1	500	500	10	.02	100	100	100	2
2	300	790	32	.041	—	100	98	4
3	—	758	58	.077	110	210	204	16
4	—	700	50	.071	—	210	188	13

The first year, from left to right, illustrates the calculation of cost depletion in the year of initial investment. In year two reserves are added, the new reserve base is calculated and cost depletion determined. In year three additional investment is added and the new investment base is determined, after which cost depletion is calculated. Note that cost depletion is always calculated from the undepleted cost (I). The example shown in Table 4–1 typifies most depletion calculations for oil and gas leases. For small companies cost depletion usually has meaning only early in the life of a property when the net income is very small or negative. As percentage depletion becomes available with income, it is usually larger than cost depletion and is therefore used instead. More on this later.

Percentage Depletion

Calculating cost depletion is only one of three calculations which must be made to determine allowable depletion. A second step is to calculate 15% of gross income. Since percentage depletion can never exceed 50% of net income from a property, the third calculation is to determine the net income from the property. A simple graph, Fig. 4–1 illustrates the relationship between cost, percentage depletion, and 50% of net income and how one determines, from these, the allowable depletion.

Calculating Net Income

In Table 4–2 the calculations necessary to find allowable depletion are illustrated. Note the determination of net income. It results from reducing gross income (revenue) by:

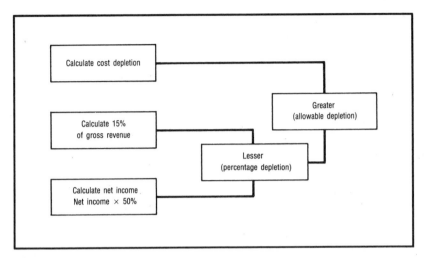

Fig. 4–1   Calculating allowable depletion

a. Operating expense of the issue.
b. Intangible drilling costs (IDC). Remember we said earlier that IDC affected the determination of percentage depletion. See also the notes on IDC, p. 40.
c. Dry hole costs on the lease.
d. Depreciation of lease and well equipment (calculated as a percentage of tangible investment).
e. Overhead for depletion limitation (calculated as a per cent of gross income).

In year one, the lease net income is negative, thus 50% of income is also negative. Since percentage depletion cannot exceed 50% of net, the 15% of gross cannot be deducted. Assuming we are dealing with the same property as in Table 4–1 we can only take cost depletion amounting to $2,000. (Remember we can always take cost depletion if to our advantage—see Fig. 4–1). Cost depletion is the allowable depletion for year one as shown in column 11, Table 4–2.

The same condition exists for year two where net income is still negative. In the third year, however, with no IDC, the income is positive and we check to see which is the smaller—15% of gross or 50% of net. Since 15% of gross is smaller (but larger than cost depletion), it becomes the allowable depletion.

Year four is similar to year three. In **both** years three and four, 50% of net is greater than percentage depletion, but by law we must take the lesser of these two numbers. Normally, it is only in the last years of

TABLE 4–2

Calculating Allowable Depletion
(Thousands of Dollars)

Yr.	1 Gr. Inc.	2 Lse. & Well Exp.	3 IDC & Dry Holes	4 L&W Depr'n.	5 Ovhd. 8%	6 Total Exp.	7 Lse. Net Inc.	8 50% of Net Inc.	9 15% of Gr. Inc.	10 Cost Dpl'n.	11 Allow. Dpl'n.
1	30	7	110	1	2	120	(90)	(45)	5	2	2
2	96	18	100	2	8	128	(32)	(16)	14	4	4
3	175	35	—	4	14	53	122	61	26	16	26
4	150	31	—	3	12	46	104	52	23	13	23

a property's life (or under conditions of very high operating costs) that the 15% is restricted by the 50% limitation. Note that columns 8, 9, and 10 contain the three separate calculations which must be compared to determine allowable depletion. Again, see Fig. 4–1.

The Timing of Deductions

We have already briefly mentioned the importance of timing in tax planning. The timing of a tax deduction refers to the year in which an expenditure may be deducted, if deducted at all. Because of ever present cash needs, a corporation usually tries to get tax deductions at the earliest practical date. Deductions save taxes; and taxes saved are the same as a return of cash to a company or at least an earlier availability of money.

Most companies with taxable income would expense all expenditures for tax purposes if permitted by the IRS. However, some expenditures must be capitalized; but even capitalized expenditures have different rates of depreciation permissible. Therefore, our next discussion will center on the timing of deductions through depreciation.

> **Definition:** *Depreciation* is a deduction from income reflecting loss of value of intangible equipment due to wear and tear. It reduces taxable income by charging (depreciating) a part of the cost against each year's income.

Computing Depreciation

Several depreciation methods are used in determining corporate income and taxable income. These methods can be grouped into four categories:

1. Straight line
2. Accelerated
   a. Declining balance
   b. Sum-of-the-Years-Digits (SYD)
3. Unit of production
4. Accelerated Cost Recovery System (ACRS)

The Straight Line Method.   The straight line method for computing depreciation deducts an equal increment each year over the life of the property.

In calculating straight line depreciation, the depreciable amount is divided by the number of years considered to be the useful life of the property. (In actual accounting practice, it is the depreciable amount less the estimated salvage value. However, in our evaluations we ignore salvage value for reasons which will be more obvious when we study the time value of money. Note, therefore, that the depreciation discussions for all methods are simplified by excluding the effect of salvage value. This simplification will not preclude sound exploratory decisions.) Dividing the depreciable amount by years of useful life, yields the annual depreciation deducted from income. For example, assume a depreciable cost of $100 and a 10-year life. The annual depreciation is:

$$\frac{100}{10} = \$10 \text{ per year for 10 years}$$

Accelerated Methods

Accelerated methods for computing depreciation apportion larger amounts of the depreciable investment to earlier years in the life of the equipment. You get a faster tax write-off—an earlier availability of money—which we have already stated is desirable. A discussion of two common methods of accelerated depreciation follows:

The Declining Balance Method.   In the declining balance method, the annual depreciation is calculated at 150% or 200% of the straight line rate applied to the undepreciated balance of the investment. For tax purposes both the 150% and 200% declining balance methods are used. The 200% rate is sometimes called the *double declining balance.* The 150% factor is applied to used equipment or new nonresidential buildings. The 200% factor is used for new equipment.

Assume the same $100 investment and the 10-year life used in the straight line method, but now we will accelerate the depreciation using the double declining balance (200% factor). The straight line method deducted 10% per year. The declining balance method (200%) will deduct 20% per year of the remaining investment. Computations for the first few years are:

First year $100 × .20 = $20
Second year ($100 − $20) × .20 = $80 × .20 = $16
Third year   ($80 − $16) × .20 = $64 × .20 = $13, etc.

Sum-of-the-Years-Digits Method (SYD).   The SYD method applies only to new equipment having a useful life of at least three years. The investment is multiplied each year by the proper SYD fraction. In this fraction the numerator is the remaining life of the equipment, as of the beginning of the year, and the denominator is the sum-of-the-digits in the total life of the equipment.

Assuming the same investment (depreciable cost) of $100 and a 10-year life, the SYD depreciation would be as follows:

Sum-of-the-year-digits equals:

$$10 + 9 + 8 + 7 + 6 + 5 + 4 + 3 + 2 + 1 = 55$$

Year	SYD Fraction	Per Cent	Depreciable Cost	Computation	Depreciation
1	10/55	18.2	100	100×.182	$18
2	9/55	16.4	100	100×.164	16
3	8/55	14.5	100	100×.145	15. . .etc.

Tax Equity and Fiscal Responsibility Act of 1982
The Economic Recovery Act of 1981

The Economic Recovery Act, passed by Congress in 1981, changed the depreciation rate for most business assets. The new law affected only those assets placed in service after December 31, 1980. It substituted an Accelerated Cost Recovery System (ACRS) for the existing rules for tax depreciation. Keep in mind, however, that the assets placed in service before 1981 still use the methods just described—i.e., straight line, double declining balance, SYD, etc. Certain provisions of the Economic Recovery Act of 1981 were modified by the Tax Equity and Fiscal Responsibility Act of 1982. The paragraphs which follow describe basic changes from both Acts which affect exploratory and development investments.

The laws placed property in one of five classes. These classes relate to the period over which full depreciation can be taken for a new investment. Under the old law, depreciation periods were based on "useful lives" established by the IRS. In general, the new periods were shorter than the useful life of the investment; thus, the title of the new depreciation, Accelerated Cost Recovery System, was most appropriate. Businesses have faster recovery of capital and therefore can temporarily defer a portion of tax on income.

The classes are:

1. Three-year property
2. Five-year property

3. Ten-year property
4. Fifteen-year public utility property
5. Fifteen-year real property

To the petroleum industry, the most important change involved tangible assets used in exploration, production, refining, marketing, pipelining, and so on. These investments fell in the five-year property category and were eligible for a 10% investment tax credit.

The depreciation schedule for the five-year property category is:

	Five-Year Property—Depreciation Rates Rate, %	
Year	Annual	Cumulative
1	15	15
2	22	37
3	21	58
4	21	79
5	21	100

To illustrate the difference in cost recovery, the following table compares straight line, double declining balance, SYD and the new rates, under ACRS, which applied to investments after 1980.

TABLE 4–3

	Straight Line		Double Declining Balance		Sum-of-Yrs-Digits		5-Year Property (ACRS)	
Year	Annual	Cumulative	Annual	Cumulative	Annual	Cumulative	Annual	Cumulative
1	$10	$10	$20	$20	$18	$18	$15	$15
2	10	20	16	36	16	34	22	37
3	10	30	13	49	15	49	21	58
4	10	40	10	59	13	62	21	79
5	10	50	8	67	11	73	21	100
6	10	60	7	74	9	82		
7	10	70	5	79	7	89		
8	10	80	4	83	5	94		
9	10	90	3	86	4	98		
10	10	100	14	100	2	100		
			100		100		100	

Total $100

At the end of the fifth year, the halfway mark, the SYD method has produced almost 50% more capital recovery through depreciation than the straight line method. In that same time the declining balance method (the 200% factor is called the double declining balance) has recovered 33% more. However, the new law (ACRS) has recovered all the investment through depreciation—100% more than the straight line method. Thus, the depreciation rate of the new law (ACRS) recovers capital the fastest of all existing systems.

Another difference between the old system and the ACRS is important. In the ACRS no salvage value must be deducted from the base for depreciation; thus, you can recover 100% of your investment through depreciation.

One additional note on the double declining balance method. In theory the double declining balance method never fully depreciates the investment. It is always depreciation of a gradually declining investment which never gets to zero. (It's akin to emptying a bottle of milk by removing one-half of the contents at each withdrawal). In Table 4–3 the number 14 in the tenth year assumes that the asset is worn out and abandoned without salvage. In this case the remaining investment can be written off. Any asset when abandoned or destroyed after being worn out can be considered fully depreciated in that year; so the undepreciated investment in year ten in the declining balance methods was assumed to be written off in year ten.

Other Changes in TEFRA

The Tax Equity and Fiscal Responsibility Act of 1982 (TEFRA) also made other changes affecting exploratory investments. These were:

1. The depreciable base for every post-1982 investment was reduced by one-half of its investment tax credit. For example, with an investment tax credit of 10%, only 95% of the investment may be recovered through depreciation.
2. For well investments after 1982, producers must reduce their intangible development costs (IDC) by 20%. This 20% must be capitalized and is recovered over a three-year period by straight line depreciation. Furthermore, an investment tax credit cannot be claimed for these capitalized amounts.
3. TEFRA repealed the tariff adjustment for the Trans-Alaska Pipeline System (TAPS). Under prior law the base price for the windfall profits tax on Sadlerochit oil was adjusted upward by the amount the average tariff per barrel (for the preceding quarter) fell below $6.26. TEFRA repealed this adjustment for Sadlerochit oil produced after December 31, 1982.
4. Rules limiting an oil company's right to credit foreign taxes against U.S. tax on the same income were changed. The effect

was to make foreign exploration expenditures nondeductible; i.e. instead of spending 66-cent dollars for foreign exploration, a company now spends 100-cent dollars.

The Tax Reform Act of 1986

Depreciation rates were again changed in 1986. A new Accelerated Cost Recovery System (ACRS) was instituted. For most petroleum investments, the period of depreciation was increased from five to eight years, obviously with lowered rates for most individual years.

A comparison of the new and old ACRS rates are:

Year	Depreciation-ACRS-%	
	1981-1986	After 1986
1	15	14.3
2	22	24.5
3	21	17.5
4	21	12.5
5	21	8.9
6		8.9
7		8.9
8		4.5
TOTAL	100	100.0

The overall effect of the tax changes in 1986 was to reduce the rate of capital recovery and raise taxable income. Because tax laws change quickly (and almost continuously) see your tax consultant to check for new legislation affecting your investment opportunity. Keeping informed about major changes influencing investment decisions will save you time in the long run.

The Unit-of-Production Method

The unit-of-production method is used to depreciate lease and well equipment that has a life largely controlled by the physical depletion of reserves. It is a similar calculation to that of cost depletion.

The amount to be deducted each year may be expressed as:

$$(C - D) \times \frac{P}{R} \text{ or } (Cost - Depreciation) \times \frac{Production\ for\ year}{Remaining\ reserve}$$

where:

C = the cost of equipment
D = accumulated depreciation
P = barrels or Mcf of gas produced during the year
R = recoverable barrels or Mcf remaining in the reservoir at
  yearend plus current year's production

An illustration of the calculation follows:

Year	C Cost of Equip.	D Prior Years Accum. Deprec.	C-D Depreciable Balance	R Reserves	P Prod.	$\frac{P}{R}$ Deprec. Rate	C-D×$\frac{P}{R}$ Annual Deprec.
1	100	—	100	40	2	.050	5
2	100	5	95	38	4	.105	10. . .etc.

Points to Remember about Depreciation

1. For tax purposes, you should take advantage of accelerated methods whenever possible.
2. You benefit substantially by increasing the rate of depreciation in the earlier years.
3. Computed by any method you get tax deductions equal to the original (depreciable) cost of the item exclusive of salvage.
4. The axiom to remember is—take the biggest deduction possible at the earliest date possible.

The Tax Treatment of
Exploratory Expenditures

There are certain basic considerations in the potential capitalization of any expenditures for tax purposes. These are:

1. Our first inquiry is always—must the expenditure be capitalized or can it be deducted as current expense?
2. If deductible, (expensed) no further tax considerations are necessary.
3. If capitalized we must ask:
   a. Must it be permanently capitalized?

   b. May all or part be deducted for tax purposes in later
      years?
   c. Will any tax benefits be derived?

As a rule of thumb for tax purposes, we should capitalize as little as possible, expense as much as possible. Of course, the application of this general rule must be within the law.

Lease Bonus

Lease bonus payments are capitalized for both booked and tax purposes. The tax laws state that the bonus on a productive lease is recovered only through the depletion allowance. For large companies, because of the Tax Reduction Act of 1975 this limits the recovery of bonus to cost depletion only. If the lease is nonproductive and surrendered, the bonus is deductible (expensed for tax purposes) in the year of surrender.

An allocated portion of lease bonus must be subtracted each year from gross income before figuring depletion, i.e., gross income for calculating taxable income is not the same as gross income (depletable income) for calculating depletion. The amount per year is usually so small that it is ignored in our evaluations. It obviously cannot be ignored for large bonuses, such as offshore sealed bid sales.

Intangible Drilling Costs

IDC must also be recovered through allowable depletion if capitalized. Herein lies the strongest motivation for expensing intangibles. If capitalized they are recovered, now mostly through cost depletion, but over the life of a property. The time delay in recovery lowers near-term cash flows and therefore is much less desirable than expensing intangibles and getting complete recovery in the year of expenditure. Thus, all companies expense as much of the IDC as allowed by the law.

Geophysical Crew Costs, Test-Well Contributions (TWC) and Core Drilling

These expenditures are expensed on the corporate books but may be capitalized or expensed for tax purposes. A company usually will expense these costs if possible.

The IRS, however, has ruled that if the information received adds value or contributes to a decision to acquire or retain acreage, the cost must be capitalized. Divergent opinions are possible in this area and discussions are often held with IRS agents to interpret results from such expenditures. Ordinarily, historic experience is used in investment evaluation to estimate capitalized geophysical crew costs. However, if these costs are a significant per cent of total exploration costs special adjustments may need to be made. It is the expensed items which receive the most careful scrutiny. Capitalized charges are not questioned by the IRS. In addition to crew costs, some data processing, interpretation (both geological and geophysical) and portions of overhead are now capitalized by IRS practice.

Trades

Trades may involve farmouts, farmins, or contributions. Tax planning for trades concerns deductions for IDC and allowable depletion if available to either party.

The tax consequences of trades can be complex. In addition, changes occur continuously as a result of legislation, court rulings, or changes in IRS regulations. For example, an IRS ruling, (77-176), made certain types of trades subject to more income tax. Because the tax consequence of trades varies considerably by virtue of the type of trade and from changing rulings and legislation, they will be discussed only in a very general manner here.

Trades vary considerably. In fact the possible variations are almost infinite. However, trades can be divided into three major classifications:

Working Interest

Full Assignment	Partial Assignment	Contribution
A. With an override retained	A. With a working interest retained	A. Dry hole money
B. Subject to a profit sharing	B. With a convertible override retained	B. Bottomhole money
	C. A carried interest agreement	C. Acreage

The full assignment relieves the assignor of most responsibilities and usually poses the fewest tax problems. Partial assignments, on the other hand, generally pose the most numerous tax problems to the assignee.

The tax consequences of trades require special study. Unless trades are quite uniform, the best advice is to consult your tax advisor or your tax department. An important reference in this area is Arthur Anderson and Company's "Oil and Gas Federal Income Tax Manual."

Tax effects must be considered carefully in trades because profitability can be materially increased by wise tax planning.

Summary

As a final resumé of all we have discussed, a table follows in which the tax treatment of exploration expenditures is compared to the booked treatment. You will find this table to be one of the most useful references in the manual.

TABLE 4–4
Summary
Tax Treatment vs. Book Treatment

	Tax Treatment	Book Treatment
1. Dry holes		
Exploratory	Expense	Expense
Development	Expense	Capitalize
2. Successful wells		
Intangible well costs	Expense (70%)	Capitalize
Tangible well costs	Capitalize	Capitalize
3. Lease bonus	Capitalize	Capitalize
4. G&G costs:		
Core drilling	Capitalize or expense	Expense
Seismic crews	Capitalize or expense	Expense
Data processing	Capitalize or expense	Expense
Interpretation	Capitalize or expense	Expense
Test well contributions	Capitalize or expense	Expense
Portion of overhead	Capitalize or expense	Expense
5. Depreciation:		
Lease and well		
equipment—new	New ACRS	Unit of production
Other equipment—new	New ACRS	Straight line
6. Depletion	Percentage or cost depletion	Cost depletion
7. Unoperated leases	Expense (as surrendered)	Amortized
8. Rentals and taxes	Expense	Expense

The word "amortized," item 7 in Table 4–4, has not been defined herein. It is somewhat akin to depreciation except it does not relate to tangible things which wear out. It relates to intangible items such as surrendered leases. It is a means of deduction, over a period of years, of the value of an expenditure which is not expensed. The amount amortized (deducted) each year is usually based on experience.

The Windfall Profit Tax

When the huge increases in wellhead oil prices occurred in the late 1970s, the Carter administration reacted with a bill to transfer any excess revenues from the increases from the petroleum industry to the federal treasury. The transfer was to be accomplished by the Windfall Profit Tax (WPT) on crude oil. It was not a tax on profits, but a tax on revenue and it was a complicated piece of legislation.

The basic philosophy behind the bill was to take all production over a given level, called the base production control level (BPCL), and subject it to a tax related to the wellhead price. In addition, numerous artificial categories of crude production were created, each with its own particular relationship to the new tax law. Further, independent producers were given lower tax rates than integrated producers. All in all, the WPT was a most complex bill.

A summary of the Windfall Profit Tax appears in Table 4–5. Tier 1 includes lower tier oil with an average initial adjusted base price of $13.06. The average initial adjusted base price is the initial price to which escalation rates were applied. As it turned out, prices did not escalate as Congress anticipated and the so-called windfalls to the industry never occurred.

The problem in this book deals with a gas discovery; as such it is not affected by the Windfall Profit Tax. Because the law is complex and base prices constantly change (because of inflation) an analyst should check with the local company expert on what prices should be projected and how they will be affected by the Windfall Profit Tax.

TABLE 4–5
Summary of the Windfall Profit Tax

Tier 1	Tax Rate Independent Producer	Other	Average Initial Base Price 3/1/80	Annual Adjust. To Base Price
Lower tier	50%	70%	$13.06	Inflation
Upper tier	50%	70%	$13.06	Inflation
new oil	50%	70%	$13.06	Inflation
marginal well	50%	70%	$13.06	Inflation
Tier 2				
Stripper well	30%	60%	$15.50	Inflation
NPR oil*	30%	60%	$15.50	Inflation
Tier 3				
new discovery oil	–	30%	$16.96	Infl. + 2%
heavy oil	–	30%	$16.96	Infl. + 2%
tertiary oil	–	30%	$16.96	Infl. + 2%

* National Petroleum Reserve Oil

The Natural Gas Policy Act of 1978

Equally as complicated as the price regulations of the Windfall Profit Tax, was the Natural Gas Policy Act of 1978. Its aim was to move prices of natural gas gradually toward deregulation. It also placed intrastate sales of natural gas under Federal control for the first time.

The Natural Gas Policy Act (NGPA) set out numerous categories of natural gas, gave them different price considerations—of initial price and escalation rates. Although most natural gas supplies were to be completely deregulated on or about January 1, 1985, the Act also selected a few categories which were not to be deregulated. On the other hand, it immediately deregulated all gas from producing zones below 15,000 feet.

The categories of gas created were new natural gas (new onshore, new reservoirs and new OCS), new onshore production wells (below 5,000 feet, above 5,000 feet), old OCS gas, high-cost gas, stripper well gas, natural gas dedicated to interstate commerce (wells spudded on or after January 1, 1975, wells spudded from January 1, 1973, to January 1, 1975, and others), gas sold under existing intrastate contracts and five or six additional categories. In other words, a highly complex bill requiring massive increases in recordkeeping. The entity that produces the bill seldom has to do the bookwork.

Because this bill is so complicated and involves so many categories of natural gas, the analyst must confer with the local expert to establish the correct price structure for his evaluation.

The sharp decline in wellhead prices and the deregulation of some categories of natural gas, during the mid-1980s, has diminished the role of the NGPA. It still must be considered for certain properties, however, and is mentioned for this reason.

REVIEW

The purpose of this chapter has been to isolate important areas of exploratory activity where proper tax treatment can reduce taxes. The subject of Federal income tax has been treated generally; and no one will become a tax expert from our discussions. I hope, however, that an awareness of potential tax savings has been gained. The explorationist should consider the effect of taxes in analyzing and comparing investment opportunities.

BIBLIOGRAPHY

1. "Impact of 1986 Tax Reform Act on Oil and Gas," *World Oil*, March 1987, pg. 56.

5 Converting Exploration Programs to Cash Flows "Cash Flow Analysis"

Previous chapters dealt with the terms and concepts needed to understand investment evaluation. This understanding of methods and terms was necessary in order to proceed with more complex methods.

Most corporations have growth as an objective. Spectacular growth can be achieved for the small company, either through merger or fortuitous investments. As a corporation gets larger, it takes increasingly larger new investments to ensure growth. Thus, every major corporation must wisely reinvest part of its profits to enable continued growth. The rate of growth becomes a test of the skill in evaluating and selecting the best new investments from the stockpile of opportunities.

Some companies are capital limited. In such cases the best investments are selected, starting at the top. Investing continues until no funds are left. For a company not capital limited, a different approach applies. In this instance minimum standards are set and all investments are made which qualify. The minimum standard must be above the cost of capital, to ensure growth; and a company's rate of growth will be determined by its ability to make a satisfactory return on new investment opportunities. Regardless of the financial ability of a corporation, it is important to compare investments on a common basis.

Large investments in high-risk ventures require careful and sound evaluation. Major corporations have the financial ability to make large investments. They also have, within reason, the capital to invest in high-risk ventures if the potential gains are worth the risk.

One of the basic tools to evaluate and compare investment opportunities is cash flow analysis. This chapter builds the basis for converting exploratory plays or programs into cash flow streams.

Cash Flow Analysis

The end result of matching the inflow and outflow of all related funds, over the life of an investment, is a *cash flow stream.*

The calculation of a cash flow stream is frequently referred to as building an economic model. Regardless of the terminology, a technique is needed to depict expenditures for investments and subsequent revenue generated. Cash flow analysis not only relates investments to subsequent revenues, but also enables a comprehendible comparison between investments.

The difference between inflows and outflows over a period of time adds up to profit or loss. This difference is called *net cash flow.* Note that we have said that the net cash flow can be positive or negative. For most investments, particularly those in the exploration department, the early annual cash flows are negative. They are negative because outflow (the money to make the investment) exceeds inflow (revenue).

One can use cash flow analysis for any entity which has both income and expense. A corporation, individual, government, club, or organization can use this principle.

The total cash flow, positive or negative, for a corporation is the sum of the cash flows for all functions. In exploration economics we look at the cash flows for the combined exploration-production investment stream. We try to analyze all opportunities on a standard basis, building our economic models as carefully and realistically as possible. As we learned in the preceding chapter, proper income tax calculations are an important facet of cash flow streams.

Our construction of a mathematical model for exploration-production investments will separate the cash flow into two segments. In so doing the tax effects on each segment can be more clearly shown. We will investigate first the investment cash flow stream (after Federal income tax); and secondly, the income cash flow stream (again, after FIT). The sum of the two streams will be the after-tax net cash flow or the profit from the investment.

The Investment Cash Flow Stream

Before we can set up our investment cash flow stream, we must break our expenditures into subgroupings for tax purposes. The separation is shown in Table 5–1 which categorizes for tax treatment the expenditures associated with the School prospect.

TABLE 5–1

Investment cash flow stream, $M
School prospect

	Year	Expenditure Type for Tax Treatment			
		Capitalized[1]	Tangible[2]	Intangible[3]	Expensed[4]
Explo.	0	500	—	—	—
	1	100	—	—	200
	2	—	—	—	1200
	3	—	200	700	100
		Exploration expenditure = $3,000			
Prod.	4	—	500	1500	300
	5	—	100	—	800
		Production expenditure = $3,200			
	Total	600	800	2200	2600
		Booked investment: $3,600		Total = $6,200	

[1] Lease acquisition and leasing cost, part of geophysical, geological, data processing and division overhead.
[2] Part of successful well costs, lease and service facilities.
[3] Part of successful well costs.
[4] Scouting, lease rentals and taxes, dry holes, overhead on investment and part of leasing, geological, geophysical and exploration overhead.

First let's deal with the exploration expenditures. Our separation isolates tangible and intangible costs for wells, capitalized exploration costs and those items which are expensed. We can follow the development of the School prospect by looking at expenditures, the category in which they are placed and the year of expenditure.

Note that the first year is given the number zero. Year zero is considered, in cash flow analysis, the point of the first significant expenditure associated with the investment being analyzed. One can start a cash flow analysis from any decision point. Downstream decision points, if evaluated, represent partial evaluations only and should be undertaken with the full knowledge that they do not reflect the entire investment. Partial evaluations are sometimes improperly called "incremental" investments. An exploratory investment made to generate a profit is actually a series of investments, each requiring a decision based on the outcome of prior investments. The prior investments were made as additional information was obtained through either more exploratory data or drilling.

Production department expenditures amount to $3.2 million, which with exploratory funds yield total out-of-pocket expenditures of $6.2 million. The capitalized investment, however, (what we show on the corporate books as an asset) amounts to only $3.6 million.

Adjusting an Investment Cash Flow Stream for Federal Income Tax

From the separations made in Table 5–1, an investment cash flow can be constructed. Remember, we are separating the investment and revenue (income) flow streams for convenience and ease of explanation only. The investment flow stream for the School prospect is shown in Table 5–2.

In year zero in Table 5–2, an expenditure of $500,000 is indicated under the column entitled "capitalized" with the subtitle "regular." The regular column is used to distinguish the type of capitalization commonly used before recent tax law changes. Current tax law requires the capitalization of 30% of the intangible development costs (IDC). The $500,000 represents lease bonus and the net outflow for year zero is a negative $500,000 or − $500,000. In year one, more leases are purchased and geophysical work is conducted on the prospect with additional exploratory expenses incurred, both adding up to $200,000.

In year three, − $210,000 appears in the 30% IDC column. It represents the first segregation of the IDC into the 70% expensed and the 30% which must be capitalized. The capital categorized as 30% IDC will be recovered in the income stream by means of straight line depreciation (shown in Table 5–4).

Note the income tax credit column in Table 5–2. It shows a plus $68,000 in year one. Where does this money come from? Remember, the tax rate is 34% and there are $200,000 of expensed items (column 5). In cash flow analysis, each investment receives credit for the income tax saved. In spending the $200,000, we incur a reduction in income tax of $68,000 and the School prospect receives credit for this amount. It shows up, then, as an inflow under the tax credit column (column 7). Please note. This procedure only has merit if a company has profits from which such deductions can be made. A company with no income from other properties could not take such a credit.

Because of the tax credit, the net cash outflow for year one is only − $232,000. We spent $300,000 but saved $68,000 in income tax. The government did not hand us $68,000, but we saved $68,000 in taxes by virtue of the $200,000 in expensed costs.

TABLE 5-2
Investment Cash Flow, $M
(After Federal Income Tax)
School Prospect

Year	1 Capitalized Regular	2 30% IDC	3 Tangible	4 70% of Intangible	5 Expense	6 Exp. + 70% of Intangible	7 Income Tax Credit*	8 Investment Cash Flow AFIT
0	−500	—	—	—	—	—	—	− 500
1	−100	—	—	—	− 200	− 200	+ 68	− 232
2	—	—	—	—	−1200	−1200	+ 408	− 792
3	—	−210	−200	− 490	− 100	− 590	+ 201	− 799
4	—	−450	−500	−1050	− 300	−1350	+ 459	−1841
5	−100	—	—	—	− 800	− 800	+ 272	− 628
Total	−700	−660	−700	−1540	−2600	−4140	+1408	−4792

*34% of Column 6

Total finding cost (BFIT) = $3,000,000 (Exploration expenditures)

Net finding cost (AFIT) = $2,323,000 (Exploration expenditures after tax credits)

Net investment (AFIT) = $4,792,000 (Exploration and production expenditures after tax credits)

Total outflow (BFIT) = $6,200,000 (Exploration & production expenditures)

In year two the $1.2 million in the intangibles and expensed column (column 6) indicates two shallow dry holes, but they generated a tax credit (inflow), so the net outflow is only − $792,000. Year three represents the last year of exploration investment. The $200,000 under the tangible column (an outflow) indicates the discovery well. As mentioned the intangible development cost is split between columns two and four, as only 70% can be expensed for tax purposes. The $490,000 of IDC (representing the 70% of total IDC—see Table 5–1) and the $100,000 of expensed items together generate tax credits of $201,000 making the net outflow for year three − $799,000.

The sum of the net cash outflow to this point represents the after-tax exploratory expenditures. They total $2.323 million. Compared to total exploratory expenditures of $3.0 million, we see the significance of the tax credits (inflows) to the investment stream. Incidentally, finding costs, expressed as dollars per barrel or cents per Mcf, are normally related to total expenditures, not the after-tax investment.

An important point is illustrated by the tax credits. When a company ceases to make new investments (fails to incur depreciation and expense deductions), its taxable income and income tax increase sharply. A liquidating company always looks good on the stockholders report because of a high return on booked assets. But the lack of new investments means it is living on borrowed time. One sees here the motivation into diversified investments where a surplus cash flow exists.

Years four and five show the outflows for production department expenditures. These outflows include the wells drilled to develop the prospect plus the necessary lease facilities (tank batteries, gathering lines, separators, etc.)

Tax credits are still taken for savings from expensed items, mostly intangible drilling costs. The after-tax production investment is $2.469 million, slightly more than the exploratory expenditures of $2.323 million. The total expenditure is still $6.2 million excluding the benefit of the income tax credits. The sum of the income tax credits (inflows) and the yearly net investment outflows yield an after-tax investment for the School prospect of $4.792 million. The total income tax credits of $1.408 million plus the after-tax investment of $4.792 million equals the total expenditure amount of $6.2 million. Again, because we have other profits from which we can deduct the tax credits gained from expensed items, our company's out-of-pocket expenditure is only $4.792 million. The magnitude of the tax credits illustrates the significant difference between before- and after-tax investments.

Before leaving the investment cash flow stream, there are several points to be re-emphasized.

1. The investment cash flow stream is most often combined, at the outset, with the income cash flow stream. It was separated here for clarification purposes.
2. Remember the zero year as the year of the first significant expenditure for the investment opportunity. One can push the zero year to any downstream investment to test the contribution to net cash flow of that partial investment. Think of the zero year as a point of decision.
3. Unit finding costs are normally expressed in total expenditure dollars, not after tax.
4. The capitalized expenditures of exploration must be separated from tangible investments (which are also capitalized). Tax calculations necessitate the separation. Tangible costs associated with drilling cost, lease facilities, flow lines, etc., will be depreciated over the life of the property. The capitalized lease bonus of nonproductive leases is expensed when the leases are cancelled or allowed to expire.
5. Watch for investments occurring later in the project life (major workovers, compression to boost pressure in semi-depleted gas reservoirs, secondary recovery drilling and equipment, etc.)
6. Try to include all real or estimated expenditures associated with an opportunity. Be as realistic as possible.
7. If you work for a major oil or gas company, a centralized group will probably supply guidelines for costs or factors difficult to isolate. If not, you must estimate them on your own. Examples are:
   - environmental or permitting delays
   - future oil and gas prices
   - overhead charges
   - tax rates

The Income Cash Flow Stream

After the successful discovery well and subsequent successful development wells go on production, both inflows and outflows of cash result. The cash inflows are:

1. Gross revenue from the sale of oil, gas, natural gas liquids, or sulfur is the basic inflow. Sometimes there is a small amount of nondepletable income from gas plants not credited to the

lease. Such sums can be ignored for exploration-production evaluations in most instances.

2. Tax credits count as inflows as explained previously. These credits result from:
   • expensed items
   • depletion
   • depreciation
3. Occasionally, an investment in one plant reduces expenses in a related or connected facility. Since this reduction represents a true savings, the new investment receives credit for the reduction.
4. Net salvage value is also a type of inflow.

Items three and four are mentioned for completeness only. They are usually ignored in exploration evaluations unless the salvage value is a high per cent of the original investment. Ignoring salvage will not ordinarily significantly affect prospect or play economics. If salvage values will affect future cash flows significantly, then the dollar amounts should be entered in the appropriate year of the cash flow stream.

The outflows resulting from a successful discovery are: (Definitions for these terms are in the preceding chapter.)

1. The royalty. It is paid to the farmer or mineral fee holder. Usually the mineral fee holder receives one-eighth or one-sixth the value of all production, sometimes more. Royalties larger than one-fourth are rare. In the special case of bidding for Federal leases on the Outer Continental Shelf, royalty can be the bid variable; or a sliding scale royalty (varying with producing rate) can be coupled with bonus as the bid variable. The basic problem carried throughout this book will deal with the more general fixed royalty situation.
2. Production and ad valorem taxes. These outflows (expenses) are state and local taxes.
3. Direct operating expenses.
4. Employee benefits.
5. Overhead above the level of lease operations.
6. Federal income tax.

Having listed the income stream inflows and outflows, an example can be presented. An income cash flow stream for the School prospect follows in Table 5–3.

TABLE 5-3
Income Cash Flow Stream, $M
School Prospect

Year	1 Gross Royalty	2 Revenue	3 Net Revenue (1-2)	4 Prod & Ad. Val Tax	5 Direct Operating Cost	6 O'head above Lease*	7 Inc. Cash Flow (BFIT) (3-4-5-6)
0-3	—	—	—	—	—	—	—
4	2900	480	2420	240	60	20	2100
5	2900	480	2420	240	60	20	2100
6	3170	530	2640	260	60	20	2300
7	3170	530	2640	260	60	20	2300
8	3170	530	2640	260	60	20	2300
9	1570	260	1310	130	30	10	1140
10	1570	260	1310	130	30	10	1140
11	1570	260	1310	130	30	10	1140
12	1570	260	1310	130	30	10	1140
13	1570	260	1310	130	30	10	1140
Total	23,160	3850	19,310	1910	450	150	16,800

* Includes employee benefit expense.

By setting up column headings, one can easily see the relationship between the inflows and outflows of the income stream. From year zero through year three, no income was generated; remember the discovery well was only completed in year three. Gross revenue begins in year four and lasts for 10 years, through year 13.

The net revenue for each year is shown in column three and results from subtracting the royalty from gross revenue. Taxes, direct operating expenses, and overhead are deducted from net revenue to get the income cash flow before Federal income tax, column seven. We started with $23.16 million which nets to $16.8 million before depreciation, depletion and Federal income tax.

From this calculation of income (BFIT), we can proceed to the determination of Federal income tax. The computations fall neatly into a few columns, as shown in Table 5.4.

Note that the column numbers on Table 5–4 continue from those on Table 5–3. The consecutive column numbers will help if you desire to combine the two tables. Column seven is repeated. From income (BFIT) surrendered leases, depletion and depreciation (including the 30% IDC) are deducted to arrive at taxable income—column eleven. (Surrendered leases were not included in the investment cash flow stream because they are a non-cash item. Cash flow measures cash changes only and surrendered leases affect only income tax on a cash flow basis.) At a 34% tax rate, the Federal income tax represents about one-third of net (before-tax) income and totals $5.01 million. However, the School prospect does not pay $5.01 million in taxes because of the tax credits shown in Table 5–2.

To get the income cash flow stream, we merely subtract column twelve (Federal income tax) from the net Income (BFIT), column seven. The result is an income cash flow stream totaling $11.79 million.

Net Cash Flow

Our cash flow analysis has proceeded from the outflow of investment dollars through revenue and the taxes they generated. We have taken advantage of an investment opportunity and have estimated its future income from production to be sold. When we combine the two streams, the investment stream and the income stream, we have the net cash flow after Federal income tax (AFIT). The combination of the two streams is shown in Table 5–5.

TABLE 5-4
Income Cash Flow Stream (AFIT), $M
School Prospect

	7	8	9	10	11	12	13
	Inc. Cash Flow (BFIT)	Surr. Leases	Deprn. & Depln.		Taxable (7-8-9-10)	Fed. Income Tax	Income Cash Flow AFIT (7-11)
Year			Regular*	30% IDC			
0-3	—	—	—	—			
4	2100	200	143	132	1625	552	1548
5	2100	200	245	132	1523	518	1582
6	2300		175	132	1993	678	1622
7	2300		125	132	2043	695	1605
8	2300		89	132	2079	707	1593
9	1140		89	—	1051	357	783
10	1140		89	—	1051	357	783
11	1140		45		1095	372	768
12	1140		—		1140	387	753
13	1140		—		1140	387	753
Total	16,800	400	1000	660	14,740	5010	11,790

* New ACRS

TABLE 5-5
Net Cash Flow (AFIT) $M

Year	Inv. Cash Flow	Inc. Cash Flow	Net Cash Flow	
			Annual	Cum.
0	– 500		– 500	– 500
1	– 232		– 232	– 732
2	– 792		– 792	–1524
3	– 799		– 799	–2323
4	–1841	1548	– 293	–2616 ——Maximum Negative Cash Flow
5	– 628	1582	954	–1662
6		1622	1622	– 40
7		1605	1605	1565 ——Cumulative cash flow becomes
8		1593	1593	3158 positive in year 7.
9		783	783	3941
10		783	783	4724
11		768	768	5492
12		753	753	6245
13		753	753	6998
Totals	–4792	11,790	6998	

Actual Value Profit = + $6,998.

The first column is the investment cash flow from Table 5–2. The income cash flow stream is from Table 5–4. The combination is shown under the heading of net cash flow (AFIT). Our goal in this chapter was to calculate the figures in this column. Note the negative numbers in the first five years. The total net cash flow is $6.998 million, the difference between the income and investment cash flow streams.

Yardsticks From Cash Flow Analysis

Three important facts will be used from the cumulative cash flow shown in the last column of Table 5–5. The *maximum negative cash flow* is one such fact. It represents, on a cumulative basis, the total amount of out-of-pocket cash. Even though the after-tax investment totals $4.792 million, we are never out that much money. The School prospect earns money beginning in the fourth year and as such we only have out-of-pocket demands of $2.616 million.

The cumulative cash flow becomes positive in the seventh year. Thus, between the sixth and seventh years, the income equals the after-tax investment and a *payout* is achieved. Payout is the second fact (yardstick) to be gained from cash flow analysis.

The third and final fact used from the last column is the total net cash flow itself. It is often called the *actual value profit*. In the following chapter (when we discuss discounting annual cash flows), the reason for this terminology will be clear. In the interim, remember that the actual value profit and the total net cash flow are the same, both annually and in total.

In Figure 5–1, these three facts (economic yardsticks) are illustrated graphically. It is a plot of the cumulative cash flow for the School prospect versus time. Note again the graphic location of the maximum negative cash flow, the total cumulative cash flow (actual value profit) and the year of payout.

One more comment about cash flow analysis. If you have to borrow the money to make the investment, then the interest paid on the borrowed money must be included in the cash flow stream. The money to repay the loan should be returned in the form of depreciation from the asset for which the money was spent. So, if money is borrowed, make sure the cash flow analysis reflects all of the effects of the loan.

Accounting Versus Cash Flow

How does cash flow analysis depict an investment differently from an accounting concept? The first fact to remember is that over the

Fig. 5–1   Cumulative net cash flow (AFIT)

long haul the result is the same; i.e., the corporate net income (AFIT) is the same as the total net cash flow. There are differences, however, and they involve timing. The differences are illustrated in Table 5–6.

The upper half of Table 5–6 illustrates on a before-tax basis the accounting concept. Although the investment is made in the first year, it is reflected in accounting records only through depreciation; (i.e., the $5,000 does not enter the cash flow stream but is deducted at $1,000 per year as the revenue flows in from that investment). Note the uniform income or booked profit shown over the five-year period. Compare this illustration with the cash flow concept. In the cash flow concept, the $5,000 investment is placed in the cash flow stream in year one; it produces a negative income of − $3,000 compared to the positive $1,000 first-year booked profit. Compare subsequent years. Note the income differences. At the conclusion of the investment, year 5, the total booked profit and the cash flow (BFIT) are the same. This sameness is the important point to remember.

Summarizing the relationship in Table 5–6, we note:

1. The accounting procedure matches booked outlays against revenue as it is produced. It illustrates the effect of an

TABLE 5-6
Accounting Concept vs. Cash Flow

Accounting Concept

Period	Investment	Revenue	Depreciation	Other Expenses	Booked Profit (before FIT)
1	5,000	2,500	1,000	500	1,000
2		2,500	1,000	500	1,000
3		2,500	1,000	500	1,000
4		2,500	1,000	500	1,000
5		2,500	1,000	500	1,000
	5,000	12,500	5,000	2,500	5,000

Cash flow

Period	Investment	Revenue	Depreciation	Other Expenses	Booked Profit (before FIT)
1	5,000	2,500		500	-3,000
2		2,500		500	2,000
3		2,500		500	2,000
4		2,500		500	2,000
5		2,500		500	2,000
	5,000	12,500		2,500	5,000

investment on the overall corporate books. Its results report earning power of the corporation to the stockholders.

2. The cash flow procedure matches outflows against inflows when the disbursement is made or cash received. Its primary use is to measure annual and cumulative cash flow and to provide a standard basis for comparing one investment with another. It places emphasis on year zero.

3. In both procedures the tax concepts are shown according to statutory requirements. As you will see in the next few paragraphs, the income tax generated by a successful investment is entered into each procedure and the taxes in total are identical for corporate and cash flow calculations.

To illustrate further the comparison between cash flow and accounting procedures, Table 5–7 was prepared. It makes the comparison for the School prospect. The first difference you will note is the timing illustrated in the first column. It shows the timing of cash outlays under accounting principles. Remember we stated that in the accounting procedure we related cash outlays to time as the income is produced. Thus, the cash outlays to be reflected on the corporate books begin as revenue is produced and are reflected through depreciation and depletion. Column one is shown only for illustration purposes and does not enter the calculation of booked net income. Note that columns four and five total $3.6 million, the same as column one.

To calculate booked net income, we begin with the income cash flow stream before Federal income tax, the same as column seven, Table 5–4. The Federal income tax in column six includes investment tax credits which are preceded by a plus sign (+). These credits and expensed items affect booked net income until the fourth year. Inflows of cash start in the fourth year and depreciation of the investment begins. Note that the depreciation plus surrendered leases totals $3.6 million, the same as the capitalized (booked) investment shown in Table 5–1.

In column six, Table 5–7, the Federal income tax of $3.602 million is the algebraic sum of $5.01 million (from Table 5–4, the income stream) and the income tax credits of $1.408 million, from Table 5–2. Column seven, booked net income or corporate profit, is calculated by subtracting columns three, four, five and six from column two. The income cash flow less expensed items, surrendered leases, depreciation and depletion, and Federal income tax equals booked net income (AFIT). In total ($6.998 million), it is the same as the net cash flow AFIT.

TABLE 5–7

Accounting Concept vs. Cash Flow, $M
School Prospect

Year	1 Cash Outlay for Booked Inv.	2 Income Cash Flow (BFIT)	3 Expense (Inv.) Items	4 Surr. Leases	5 Booked Depl'n & Deprec.*	6 FIT	7 Booked Net Inc. (Profit)	8 Net Cash Flow
0	600							−500
1			200			+68	−132	−232
2			1200			+408	−792	−792
3	900		100			+34	−66	−799
4	2000	2100	300	200	400	−408	792	−293
5	100	2100	800	200	400	−238	462	954
6		2300			439	−633	1228	1622
7		2300			438	−633	1229	1605
8		2300			438	−633	1229	1593
9		1140			217	−314	609	783
10		1140			217	−314	609	783
11		1140			217	−313	610	768
12		1140			217	−313	610	753
13		1140			217	−313	610	753
Total	3600	16,800	2600	400	3200	−3602	6998	6998

* Modestly simplified for illustration purposes.

The yearly difference results from the difference in time of deductions caused by depreciation. Columns seven and eight allow a direct comparison between booked net income (corporate profit) and the net cash flow for the School prospect.

A final illustration of the accounting concept versus net cash flow is shown in Figure 5–2. The total cumulative cash flow is the same as total corporate profit. The corporate books, however, show a much different plot on a cumulative profit; for example, the maximum negative profit is only $990,000 compared to a true maximum negative cash flow of $2.616 million.

The comparisons in Figure 5–2 illustrate how accounting records reflect the return of cash versus the true picture shown by cash flow analysis. The difference is not surprising, however, when the purpose of each is understood. The corporate books reflect the extinguishing of an investment coincident with its produced revenue. Accounting principles (set forth by the Financial Accounting Standards Board) match depreciation to the revenues produced by the depreciated investment.

Cash flow analysis, on the other hand, focuses on the available cash, or lack of it, caused by a specific investment. It is an evaluative

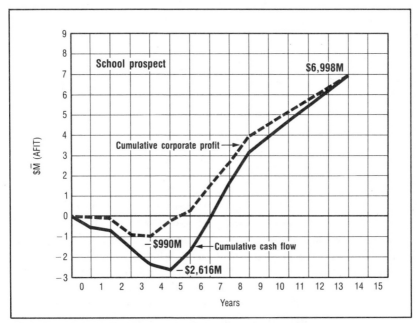

Fig. 5–2   Cumulative corporate profit vs. cash flow

tool. Chapter seven will illustrate this concept more fully. It is now enough to know that cash flow analysis is a useful tool for selecting the best investments when there are many investments from which to choose.

Book Return on Investments

The rate of return on booked net assets is a common financial yardstick. It is not often used in investment evaluation. In certain instances, however, it is desirable, particularly in a major investment, to know the effect on the corporate return of an investment opportunity. Table 5–8 illustrates the calculation of this yardstick for the School prospect.

The annual rate of return on booked investment is calculated by relating yearly booked net income (corporate profit) to the average booked investment. The average investment is calculated by dividing by two the sum of the beginning investment and the investment booked at the end of the year. Changes during the year—additions to investment and depreciation of existing investment—are reflected in the end of the year booked investment.

When used for investment evaluation, the yardstick sought is the return over the life of the investment. It is calculated as follows:

$$\text{Booked rate of return} = \frac{\text{Cumulative booked net income} \times 100}{\text{Sum of average annual booked investments}}$$

For the School prospect, this calculation is:

$$\frac{6,998}{14,988} \times 100 = 46.7\%$$

For the School prospect the booked return on investment is 46.7% for the overall project life. Note, however, that the booked return calculation enables a return on investment on an annual basis. Also of importance is the fact that the booked return, on an annual basis, increases sharply as the assets are depreciated. In the final year, the booked return is 559.6%. The most negative year was year two when the return was −132.0%. Several "return" yardsticks do not have an annual return calculation possible, as we shall see in the next chapter.

TABLE 5-8
Booked Return on Investment*
School Prospect
(Thousands of Dollars)

	1	2	3	4	5	6	7
	Cash Outlay for Bk.Inv.	Booked Depr'n & Depl'n	Investments		Avg. for Year	Booked Net Income	Booked Return on Assets
Year			Beg. of Year	End of Year			
1	600		500	600	550	−132	−24.0
2			600	600	600	−792	−132.0
3	900		600	1500	1050	−66	−6.3
4	2000	**600	1500	2900	2200	792	36.0
5	100	**600	2900	2400	2650	462	17.4
6		439	2400	1961	2180	1228	56.3
7		438	1961	1523	1742	1229	70.6
8		438	1523	1085	1304	1229	94.2
9		217	1085	868	976	609	62.3
10		217	868	651	760	609	80.1
11		217	651	434	542	610	112.5
12		217	434	217	325	610	187.6
13		217	217	—	109	610	559.6
Total	3600	3600			14,988	6998	

$$\text{Booked ROR} = \frac{6998}{14988} \times 100 = 46.7\%$$

* Successful efforts accounting method

** $400,000 in surrendered leases, $200,000 in each of the years four and five

REVIEW

Chapter 5 is one of the key building blocks in the series. Having digested the necessary terms and tax concepts, cash flow analysis can be introduced. Pertinent points from this chapter are:

1. A company grows based upon its investment opportunities and its skill in selecting the best investments from those available.
2. Cash flow analysis is a method of matching inflows and outflows. It is the first step in investment evaluation. The net cash flow is the algebraic sum of inflows and outflows.
3. Any investment is, in economic reality, a purchase of a series of future annual cash flows. Cash flow analysis is the technique by which these flows are determined.
4. The total net cash flow from an investment is exactly equal to the total net corporate profit. Annually, however, cash flow differs from corporate profit because of depreciation.
5. Three important factors are developed from cumulative net cash flow—namely, the payout period, the maximum negative cash flow and the total net cash flow.

A PROBLEM

At this point, you may want to test what you have learned. A brief problem follows; work it to see if you have adequately learned the terms and concepts to this point. The problem emphasizes the investment flow stream and the net cash flow stream. In addition to the necessary data to work the problem, two handy worksheets are included to make your calculations easier. The solution is shown in Appendix B.

CHRONOLOGY OF A SUCCESSFUL PROSPECT

Problem 1
Year 0: Good geological lead results in lease purchase.
Year 1: Geophysical work confirms prospect.
Year 2: Additional acreage leased.
Year 3: Wildcat test of prospect results in new field discovery.
Year 4: Development wells drilled; lease production facilities installed.

Year 5: Dry development well drilled. Field fully developed.

Year 15: Reserve depleted. Field abandoned.

TABLE 5–9

Required Investment*

Item	Amount ($M)	Year Incurred
Lease bonus	200	0
Additional lease bonus	50	2
Geophysical work	50	1
	(80% capitalized)	
Lease rental (1st year)	10	1
Lease rental (2nd year)	10	2
Discovery wildcat	300	3
	(70% intangible)	
Development wells	1,000	4
	(60% intangible)	
Lease facilities	200	4
Dry hole	**200	5

* Geological, scouting, overhead, etc. expenses not to be considered in this problem.
** Is it necessary to know per cent intangible for this item?

TABLE 5-10
Investment Cash Flow Stream

Year	Capitalized (1)	Tangible (2)	Intangible (3)	Expensed (4)	Total Col. 3&4 (5)	FIT Credit (6)	AFIT Investment (7)	Year	Remarks
0								0	
4								1	
2								2	
3								3	
4								4	
5								5	

TABLE 5–11
Successful Prospect
Net Cash Flow

Year	AFIT investment	Net income	Net cash flow	Cumulative net cash flow
	$M	$M	$M	
0		—		
1		—		
2		—		
3		—		
4		300		
5		500		
6		500		
7		500		
8		500		
9		500		
10		500		
11		500		
12		500		
13		300		
14		300		
15		100		

Maximum negative cash flow in year _____
Cumulative cash flow becomes positive during year _____
Payout in year _____
Total after-tax investment: $M _____
Actual value profit: $M_____

6 Tomorrow's Dollars Today (Present Value Concepts)

The concept of present value is one of the most valuable tools in investment evaluation, but definitely not the only tool. It is not a cure-all, but must be used with a thorough understanding of its advantages and limitations. Present value concepts must also be used in conjunction with other economic concepts for meaningful comparisons of investment opportunities.

You have heard the terms "discounted cash flow," "rate of return," and "present value profit." If you haven't previously been exposed to the basic principles of present values, these terms may seem shrouded by an aura of mystery. However, there is nothing new, magical or mysterious about present value economics. In fact the principles we shall discuss have been used by bankers and insurance men since "dealing in dollars" became a business. So, before we talk about present value principles, applied to the oil industry, let's talk a bit about the money business.

Interest

What makes the money business work is interest. The ability of invested funds to earn interest makes the money business a profitable one. The exact amount of interest earned is a function of two things:

1. The interest rate (i.e., 4½%, 6%, 8½%, etc.).
2. The frequency of compounding (annually, quarterly, daily, etc).

Throughout this chapter, for simplicity's sake, we will be talking only about interest compounded annually. Although more frequent compounding does make a difference, it does not significantly affect

84

exploratory investment analysis. See Appendix C for some comments on compounding at faster than annual rates.

Future Value of Invested Dollars

Let's now look at how interest acts to increase the value of money over a period of time. Suppose we have a dollar to invest; furthermore, we know where it can be invested at 10% compounded annually. We will invest our dollar now and call this point in time—year zero. After one year (year one), our money is worth:

$$(\$1.00) \ + \ (0.10) \ (\$1.00) \ = \ \$1.10 \qquad \text{(Eq. 6–1)}$$

Our dollar has earned 10 cents during its first year of investment. We can state Eq. 6–1 another way by factoring out the ($1.00). It then becomes:

$$(\$1.00) \ (1 \ + \ 0.10) \ = \ \$1.10 \qquad \text{(Eq. 6–2)}$$

In the second year, we earn interest on our original investment of $1.00 and also on the $0.10 interest earned in year one. At the end of two years, we have:

$$(\$1.10) \ + \ (0.10) \ (\$1.10) \ = \ \$1.21 \text{ or restated} \qquad \text{(Eq. 6–3)}$$

$$(\$1.10) \ (1 \ + \ 0.10) \ = \ (1.10)^2 \ = \ \$1.21 \qquad \text{(Eq. 6–4)}$$

Likewise, if our dollar remains invested for 10 years at 10% interest compounded annually, we would have $2.59 or 2.59 times our original investment.

The steps just enumerated are shown in Table 6–1. Several pertinent facts come from Table 6–1.

1. During the seventh year, our original investment doubles.
2. The equation for compounding our investment utilizes the number of the year as an exponent.

From the illlustration, we can show how the growth of any investment at any interest rate can be determined:

If: i = interest rate

n = number of years at interest i compounded annually

1 = the investment

Then: The future value of today's investment equals:

$$(\text{Investment}) \ (1 \ + \ i)^n \ \text{or}$$
$$FV \ = \ I(1 \ + \ i)^n \qquad \qquad (\text{Eq. } 6-5)$$

Equation 6–5 can be used to calculate the future value of an investment of any size. Problem 6–1 at the end of the chapter will test your understanding of this point.

TABLE 6–1

Future Value of $1.00 Invested at 10%

Years hence	Amount of 1 (Invested @ 10% rate)
0	1.00
1	$(1.00) \ + \ (1.00)(.10) \ = \ (1.00)(1 \ + \ .10) \ = \ (1.00)(1.10) \ = \ 1.10$
2	$(1.10)(1.10) \ = \ (1.10)^2 \ = \ 1.21$
3	$(1.21)(1.10) \ = \ (1.10)^3 \ = \ 1.33$
4	$(1.10)^4 \ = \ 1.46$
5	1.61
6	1.77
7	1.95
8	2.14
9	2.36
10	$2.59 \ = \ (1.10)^{10} \ = \ (1 \ + \ .10)^{10} \ ...\text{etc.}$

The Rule of 72

An interesting and useful rule of thumb (dealing with compounding) is called the "Rule of 72." Divide the number 72 by your interest rate and the answer is the number of years it takes to double your investment. For example, 10% compounded annually, will double your investment in 7.2 years. An investment at 8%, compounded annually, will double your investment in nine years. You will find this simple rule of thumb most useful in looking at your own investments or others that you may review. Try it.

The Present Value of Future Dollars

Let's look at the money business from another angle. Suppose we don't want to invest a whole dollar at 10%—but some amount less. We want our money to grow, through interest, to be worth one dollar at the end of one year. We ask ourselves a different question. How much must we invest now to have one dollar at year-end? Mathematically, we are asking:

What number $\times$ 1.10 = $1.00?

The number we are looking for is our investment, so the equation becomes:

$$I \times (1.10) = \$1.00$$

or

$$I = \frac{\$1.00}{1.10} = \$0.909 \qquad \text{(Eq. 6–6)}$$

Equation 6–6 tells us—if we invest 90.9¢ for one year at 10%, we will have a dollar at year-end. Stating this thought another way—today's value of next year's dollar (at 10%) is $0.909. A dollar of income received next year is worth only 90.9¢ today because of the loss of one year's interest at 10%.

Next let's consider the same problem, only now we want our investment to grow to a dollar in two years.

$$I(1 + 0.10)(1 + 0.10) = 1.00$$
$$I(1.10)^2 = I(1.21) = 1.00$$

$$I = \frac{1.00}{1.21} = 0.826 \qquad \text{(Eq. 6–7)}$$

Equation 6–7 tells us that if we can earn 10% compounded annually, we need only invest $0.826 to have one dollar in two years.

In investment analysis the today's value of future dollars is called the *present value;* and Equation 6–7 is usually written:

$$PV = \frac{1.00}{1.21} = 0.826$$

It would be read—that the present value of one, discounted at 10% for two years, is 0.826. This concept can be illustrated by Table 6–2.

An equation also expresses the present value concept. It develops in a way similar to Eq. 6–5. Using the tenth year as an illustration:

The present value of 1,
discounted at 10% for 10 years $= \dfrac{1}{(1 + 0.10)^{10}} = \dfrac{1}{2.59} = 0.386$

TABLE 6–2

Present Value of 1, Discounted at 10%

Years hence	Present value of 1 (Discounted @ 10% rate)
0	1.000
1	$(1.00) \div (1 + .10) = (1.00) \div (1.10) = 0.909$
2	$(1.00) \div (1.10)^2 = (1.00) \div (1.21) = 0.826$
3	$(1.00) \div (1.10)^3 = (1.00) \div (1.33) = 0.751$
4	0.683
5	0.621
6	0.564
7	0.513
8	0.467
9	0.424
10	0.386 ... etc.

So if:

i = discount rate

n = number of years discounted at rate i

Then:

$$\text{PV of } 1 = \frac{1}{(1 + i)^n} \qquad \text{(Eq. 6–8)}$$

The message from Table 6–2 is—if you can invest your money today at any interest rate, then tomorrow's dollars are worth less than a dollar today. The table shows the discount factors for the 10% discount rate. Note how rapidly the value of future dollars diminishes. By the tenth year they are worth (today) only $0.386. Note also in year zero, Table 6–2 the 1.000 figure. This number symbolizes the fact that a dollar in the pocket today is worth one dollar—Not more or less.

In Table 6–3 the discount factors are shown for eleven different discount rates, ranging from one to 50%. You will recognize the first few factors shown under the 10% discount rate.

Discounting a Cash Flow

It was necessary to go through the preceding steps to enable us to comprehend discounting. One of the steps taken in investment evaluation is to discount a cash flow stream. When discounting a flow of cash to present value, we make two assumptions:

1. In making an investment we are, in effect, purchasing a series of annual future incomes.

TABLE 6–3

Present Value of 1

$$\frac{1}{(1 + i)^n}$$

Years hence						Discount Rate					
	1%	3%	5%	6%	7%	10%	15%	20%	30%	40%	50%
1	.990	.971	.952	.943	.935	.909	.870	.833	.769	.714	.667
2	.980	.943	.907	.890	.873	.826	.756	.694	.592	.510	.444
3	.971	.915	.864	.840	.816	.751	.658	.579	.455	.364	.296
4	.961	.888	.823	.792	.763	.683	.572	.482	.350	.260	.197
5	.951	.863	.784	.747	.713	.621	.497	.402	.269	.186	.132
6	.942	.837	.746	.705	.666	.564	.432	.335	.207	.133	.088
7	.933	.813	.711	.665	.623	.513	.376	.279	.159	.095	.059
8	.923	.789	.677	.627	.582	.467	.327	.233	.123	.068	.039
9	.914	.766	.645	.592	.544	.424	.284	.194	.094	.048	.026
10	.905	.744	.614	.558	.508	.386	.247	.162	.073	.035	.017
11	.896	.722	.585	.527	.475	.350	.215	.135	.056	.025	.012
12	.887	.701	.557	.497	.444	.319	.187	.112	.043	.018	.008
13	.879	.681	.530	.469	.415	.290	.163	.093	.033	.013	.005
14	.870	.661	.505	.442	.388	.263	.141	.078	.025	.009	.003
15	.861	.642	.481	.417	.362	.239	.123	.065	.020	.006	.002
16	.853	.623	.458	.394	.339	.218	.107	.054	.015	.005	.002
17	.844	.605	.436	.371	.317	.198	.093	.045	.012	.003	.001
18	.836	.587	.416	.350	.296	.180	.081	.038	.009	.002	.001
19	.828	.570	.396	.331	.277	.164	.070	.031	.007	.002	
20	.820	.554	.377	.312	.258	.149	.061	.026	.005	.001	
21	.811	.538	.359	.294	.242	.135	.053	.022	.004	.001	
22	.803	.522	.342	.278	.226	.123	.046	.018	.003	.001	
23	.795	.507	.326	.262	.211	.112	.040	.015	.002		
24	.788	.492	.310	.247	.197	.102	.035	.013	.002		
25	.780	.478	.295	.233	.184	.092	.030	.010	.001		
26	.772	.464	.281	.220	.172	.084	.026	.009	.001		
27	.764	.450	.268	.207	.161	.076	.023	.007	.001		
28	.757	.437	.255	.196	.150	.069	.020	.006	.001		
29	.749	.424	.243	.185	.141	.063	.017	.005			
30	.742	.412	.231	.174	.131	.057	.015	.004			
31	.735	.400	.220	.164	.123	.052	.013	.004			
32	.727	.388	.210	.155	.115	.047	.011	.003			
33	.720	.377	.200	.146	.107	.043	.010	.002			
34	.713	.366	.190	.138	.100	.039	.009	.002			
35	.706	.355	.181	.130	.094	.036	.008	.002			
36	.699	.345	.173	.123	.088	.032	.007	.001			
37	.692	.335	.164	.116	.082	.029	.006	.001			
38	.685	.325	.157	.109	.076	.027	.005	.001			
39	.678	.316	.149	.103	.071	.024	.004	.001			
40	.672	.307	.142	.097	.067	.022	.004	.001			
41	.665	.298	.135	.092	.062	.020	.003	.001			
42	.658	.289	.129	.087	.058	.018	.003				
43	.652	.281	.123	.082	.055	.017	.002				
44	.645	.272	.117	.077	.051	.015	.002				
45	.639	.265	.111	.073	.048	.014	.002				
46	.633	.257	.106	.069	.044	.012	.002				
47	.626	.249	.101	.065	.042	.011	.001				
48	.620	.242	.096	.061	.039	.010	.001				
49	.614	.235	.092	.058	.036	.009	.001				
50	.608	.228	.087	.054	.034	.009	.001				

2. Future incomes can in turn be invested in other income generating activities.

These two assumptions are important. Through reinvestment any income received early has more value than later income. If the discount rate is said to be the interest rate that can be earned through reinvestment, we can use discount factors to compare values of income dollars at various points in time.

Early in the life of an investment (remember the School Prospect), the annual cash flows are most often negative. In discounting a cash flow stream, the negative values are discounted also. Why? Because we assume that until investment funds are required, that money is invested elsewhere at a rate equal to the discount rate.

Perhaps by now you are catching a glimpse of the importance of the discount rate and the timing of investments. We are about to clarify the concept of the time value of money. Let's re-examine Table 6–3. We will take a few numbers from this table and construct a new one to illustrate the signficance of various discount rates—with time.

TABLE 6–4

Comparing Factors From Present Value of 1

Years hence	Actual value (undiscounted)	Discount rate		
		5%	10%	20%
0	1.000	1.000	1.000	1.000
1	1.000	.952	.909	.833
5	1.000	.784	.621	.402
10	1.000	.614	.386	.162
20	1.000	.377	.149	.026

A comparison of present value is made for the zero year and years 5, 10, and 20. Note the undiscounted value. It will henceforth be called the *actual value.* In Table 6–4, it is always 1.000 and it is always 1.000 for any discount rate in the zero year.

Check the 10-year line. At 5% money ten years hence is worth only 0.614 per dollar. Compare the 20% rate. In the 10th year a dollar is only worth $0.162 if you could have invested it at 20%. In the 20th year at a 20% discount rate, a dollar has a value of only $0.026.

The effect of discounting is shown graphically in Fig. 6–1. Note first how fast the discount factor decreases at high rates, such as 50%. To compare the effect of various rates on a cash flow stream, start at the left of Fig. 6–1 on the 0.1 discount factor line. (Think of this factor

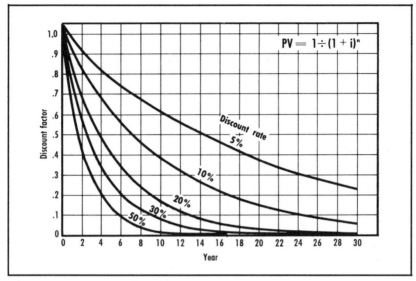

Fig. 6–1   Present value of 1

as a dollar worth 10 cents.) Moving to the right, check the intersection with each discount rate curve. At 50% by the sixth year, income flow is discounted below 10 cents. At 30% the 10-cent line is reached in 9 years, at 20% in 13 years. These curves demonstrate an important fact. Any event beyond the 10th year in a cash flow stream (inflow or outflow) has little effect on present value profit at rates higher than 20%. Even at a 10% discount rate, the significance of investments or revenues is sharply reduced beyond 10 years.

Now, to discount a cash flow. We shall use the School Prospect for our series of annual cash flows. In Table 6–5 you will recognize the cash flow stream of the School Prospect and in column 2 the 10% discount factors. These factors are multiplied times the numbers in column 1 to get the present value of the cash flow discounted at 10%. Note that no discounting takes place in year zero. Today's dollar is worth a dollar. As mentioned earlier, both negative and positive values are discounted. There is a unique discount factor for each year's annual cash flow. After each annual cash flow is discounted by its unique discount factor, the discounted annual cash flows are summed to show the present value at 10% of the entire cash flow stream. The total for the School prospect is $2.254 million as compared with the actual value of $6.998 million.

TABLE 6-5
Discounting a Net Cash Flow Stream
School Prospect

Year	1 Net cash Flow (AFIT) $ M	2 Disc. Factors 10% Rate	3 Present Value Disc. @10%	4 Disc. Factors 20% Rate	5 Present Value Disc. @20%	6 Disc. Factors 30% Rate	7 Present Value Disc. @30%
0	-500	1.000	-500	1.000	-500	1.000	-500
1	-232	.909	-227	.833	-193	.769	-178
2	-792	.826	-654	.694	-550	.592	-469
3	-799	.751	-600	.579	-463	.455	-364
4	-293	.683	-200	.482	-141	.350	-103
5	+954	.621	592	.402	+384	.269	256
6	1622	.564	915	.335	+543	.207	336
7	1605	.513	823	.279	448	.159	255
8	1593	.467	744	.233	371	.123	196
9	783	.424	332	.194	152	.094	74
10	783	.386	302	.162	127	.073	57
11	768	.350	269	.135	104	.056	43
12	753	.319	240	.112	84	.043	32
13	753	.290	218	.093	70	.033	25
Total	6998 (Actual Value Profit)		2254 (Present Value Profit)		436 (Present Value Profit)		-340 (Present Value Profit)

Column three tells us, if we have alternate investments at 10%, that the present value of future incomes from the School prospect is worth $2.254 million; or the School prospect will provide a 10% return on its cash flow stream plus an additional $2.254 million.

In column one, note the years one and four. Both have a negative cash flow of $200,000. However, when discounted at 10% these two identical numbers (on an actual value basis) are not the same. In year one the $200,000 is discounted to $182,000 and in year four it is discounted to $137,000. Why? The reason is simple. Because we do not need the second $200,000 until year four, we assume it is at work somewhere earning 10%. Thus, it is discounted more (i.e. penalized less) because it is earning money until needed. The fact that each year has its own unique discount factor means that identical annual cash flows will have different discounted cash flows for each different set of discount factors—for each different discount rate.

In column four the 20% discount factors are shown. If they are multiplied times the annual net cash flows of the School prospect (column one), the summed result is $436,000. Column five shows the results for the individual years, plus the sum. The smaller factors of 20% (higher discounting) reduce the present value profit. Column five tells us that if we have alternate investments at 20%, then the School prospect will return 20% plus $189,000.

Column six contains the discount factors for 30%. Note how much smaller these numbers are than the 10% factors. The factor for the 13th year at 10% is 0.290 compared with 0.033 for the 30% rate. The smaller factors mean more severe discounting. In fact, the discount factors are so small that the annual cash flows in column one, when discounted at 30%, sum to a negative $364,000. If we have other investments at 30%, the School prospect is a less attractive investment.

Two points can be observed from our discounting thus far. First, as the discount rate is increased, the present value profit becomes smaller and smaller and eventually becomes negative. Second, you perhaps can already envision one of the uses of this tool. If you set a target discount rate, then two separate cash flows (e.g. two prospects' cash flows) can be discounted at that rate. The one having the largest present value is the better investment (based only on this one yardstick).

Constructing A Present Value Profile

We are now ready for another quantum leap in our investment

knowledge. We have proceeded far enough to be able to construct a present value profile. It is one of the most useful of all evaluating tools.

Again, our example will be the School prospect. The present value profile for the School prospect is shown in Fig. 6–2. On such a graph, the present value is plotted for various discount rates. The discount rate is usually the horizontal axis—the present value, the vertical axis.

Note the 0% discount point in Fig. 6–2. Here, you will recognize the now familiar actual value profit (AVP) of $6.998 million. Remember, this number is the undiscounted net cash flow. Move to the 10% discount rate on the horizontal axis. Again, you see a familiar number, $2.254 million—originally shown as the total of column 3 in Table 6–5. Next, check the present value at 20%. This point also is from Table 6–5. The PVP at 20% is $436,000. Likewise, the 30% point is also from Table 6–5 and is shown as a negative number, below the zero present value profit line.

A present value profile is constructed by taking a cash flow stream and discounting it at several discount rates. At least one discount rate must produce a negative number. The various PVPs are connected as shown in Fig. 6–2. The curve which these points produce is called the *present value profile*.

Two other points can be observed from Fig. 6–2. First, note where the profile crosses the zero PVP line. At this point the discount rate is just large enough to discount the net cash flow stream to zero; i.e., the sum of the discounted negative and positive annual incomes is exactly zero. This point is called the *discounted cash flow rate* (DCFR). The DCFR for the School prospect is 24.5%. The DCFR also has other names. In a few computer programs, it is designated as the IIR or the investor's interest rate. It has been called the IRR or internal rate of return. Second, note that the profile goes below the zero present value line. For discount rates larger than 24.5%, the resulting PVPs are negative. What this fact tells us is this—if we can invest money at amounts greater than 24.5% we would, in most instances, be better off to take such investments rather than the School prospect. However, as we shall see in the next chapter, there could be investments with DCFRs greater than 24.5% that are not necessarily better than the School prospect.

Review of Figure 6–2

1. A present value profile is a plot of the PVPs resulting from discounting a net cash flow stream at various rates.
2. Three important features of the profile help us in investment evaluation. they are:

Fig. 6–2   Construction of present value profile and determination of DCFR

    a. The magnitudes of the actual value profit and present value profits at commonly quoted discount rates.
    b. The shape of the profile.
    c. The discounted cash flow rate (DCFR).
  3. The discounted cash flow rate is that rate which causes a net cash flow stream to be discounted to zero. The DCFR may also be thought of as the rate which causes the sum of the discounted outflows and inflows to equal the net cash outlay in year zero. (Remember year zero is undiscounted).

Calculating a DCFR

The discounted cash flow rate must be calculated by trial and error. It can also be determined graphically as shown in Fig. 6–2.

In most corporations, computer programs are available to calculate the DCFR. You may occasionally be faced with the need to calculate it manually with a desk calculator, adding machine, or slide rule. Where do you start? What discount rate should you first apply to the net cash flow stream? A very useful rule of thumb aids us here.

The reciprocal of payout in years times 100 is often close to the DCFR, especially for projects with equal annual cash flows. For example, if the cumulative cash flow shows payout in the fifth year, try 20% as your first discount rate:

$$\frac{1}{\text{Payout}} \times 100$$

$$\frac{1}{5} \times 100 = 20$$

If the PV at 20% is negative, you have used too large a discount. Try a smaller discount rate; do this until you have a positive PV. Three points (discount rates) are usually enough to determine the DCFR graphically. Plot the three points as in Fig. 6–2 and where the curve crosses the zero line of PV, read the DCFR.

Another Method of Viewing the DCFR

One can also view the discounted cash flow rate as the maximum interest rate which could be paid on borrowed capital and still break even.

Consider the following example. We have said that an investment yielding a 20% DCFR would allow us to borrow money at that rate and break even. This concept is illustrated in Table 6–6.

In column 1 the after-tax net cash flow shown in column 2 is discounted at 20%. The sum of the annual discounted values is zero, indicating a DCFR of 20%. Note in year zero that we borrow $3,000 which is undiscounted. Switch your attention now to the interrelationship between columns 2, 3, 4, and 5.

Our investment starts off with a negative cash flow of $3,000. In year one it earns $1,000. We pay $600 interest (column 3), apply $400 on the principal (column 4) and have an unpaid balance of $2,600 (column 5). In year two, our cash flow is again $1,000. Again we pay interest at 20% and apply some money to the principal. Our unpaid balance goes down each year, finally to zero in year six. Our cash flow was sufficient to pay off the $3,000 note and also to pay interest on the unpaid balance at the rate of 20%. The amount of interest paid was $2,030, equal to our after-tax net cash flow. We are making the assumption in this illustration that tax credits from interest paid have been taken into account in column 2, the net cash flow.

If we had paid a higher rate of interest, our cash flow would have been exceeded. A lower rate of interest would have yielded extra cash flow; so the DCFR represents the maximum interest we could pay on borrowed money and still break even on the investment.

The Reinvestment Controversy

The DCFR results from trial and error discounting of a net cash flow stream. It is often referred to as the internal rate of return because the rate is "internal" to the project. For this reason you will find references in the literature which state that the reinvestment of future cash flows does not need to be considered when using DCFR.

TABLE 6–6
The Concept of a Discounted Cash Flow Rate

Year	1 Present Value Disc. @ 20%	2 After-tax Net Cash Flow	3 Interest @ 20% on Unpaid Balance	4 Payment to Reduce Principal	5 Unpaid Balance
0	−3,000	−3,000	—	—	−3,000
1	833	1,000	−600	400	−2,600
2	694	1,000	−520	480	−2,120
3	579	1,000	−424	576	−1,544
4	482	1,000	−309	691	−853
5	402	1,000	−172	828	−25
6	10	30	−5	25	0
	0	2,030	−2,030	3,000	
(20% DCFR)					

However, such is not the case. Granted the discounting to zero is internal to the investment—but once you use DCFR to compare to another investment you have automatically made the reinvestment assumption. Pollack[4] (1961) showed convincingly that in comparing investments the reinvestment assumption is made.

Why is this controversy important? It is important because of the loss of validity of very high DCFR's. If your company investments average 12% return, then DCFRs of 60 to 80% are unrealistic in that you do not have multiple opportunities to reinvest at such high rates.

Nevertheless, the controversy does not take away the value of a high DCFR as reflecting a quick payout and a fast return of your investment. We shall see in the next chapter some attempts to develop yardsticks which compensate for this flaw of the DCFR.

Comparison of DCFR and Booked Return

Comparisons are often made between rates of return calculated by various means. In an accounting sense, rates of return are returns related to net assets or stockholders' equity, etc.

The DCFR is not a rate of return in that sense. It emphasizes the timing of inflows and outflows to a greater extent than does a return on net assets.

For most evaluations the booked rate of return will be larger than the DCFR. For the School prospect:

- the booked return was 46.7%
- the DCFR was 24.5%

As development costs increase, the rates tend to converge near the same value. There are numerous references in the literature to other rates of return and evaluation methods.[1,2,3] New concepts in evaluation should be expected to emerge as new needs appear and better methods are discovered to describe investment opportunities. As will be shown in the next chapter, evaluation techniques and yardsticks are still evolving.

The best way to compare the DCFR and a return on net assets is to note their intent. A return on assets measures the profit over a period as related to the capitalized investments. It is a standard business method common to all profit making organizations. The DCFR is not a return on assets. Its intent is to help in the comparison between investments. It measures their cash flow relative to year zero on a common basis, not their assets. These differences allow a generalization about the two terms. The DCFR is for evaluation purposes to help (with other yardsticks) choose the best investment. A return on assets reports, in standard accounting concepts, the money earned by a firm's assets. The two terms are distinctly individual in nature and intent and are not comparable.

A Method Showing The Rough Relationship Between DCFR and Return on Net Assets

A method does exist to illustrate the indirect manner in which both DCFR and return on net assets are related. It is shown in Table 6–7. Table 6–7 begins with the same basic information shown earlier in Table 5–6. The upper portion shows a BFIT calculation of return on net assets. The beginning and end-of-the-year investments are shown plus the corporate profit at $1,000 per year. Remember the number $1,000 is not the actual cash flow. The cash inflow (revenue after expenses) is $2,000 per year, the difference between it and the corporate profit being the $1,000 per year of depreciation. Relating the total corporate profit ($5,000) to the average investment over the life of the project yields a return on net assets of 40%. The numerator, to make this calculation, is the $5,000 divided by the sum of the average annual net assets, $12,500, shown in the last column of the upper portion of Table 6–7.

To show how a DCFR is indirectly related to assets, first calculate the DCFR. To make the calculation the cash flow of Table 5–6 (lower portion) is discounted to zero—resulting in a DCFR of 28.6%. In the lower section of Table 6–7, the beginning-of-the-year (BOY) investment is assumed always to earn 28.6%. As the BOY investment decreases, so do the earnings from $1,433 in year one to $444 in year five. Total earnings are the same $5,000 as the corporate profit. Please note. The assumption of earnings each year at a flat rate of 28.6% on the BOY investment does not reproduce, on an annual basis, the actual cash flow, as shown in Table 6–8. It does reproduce the total BFIT cash flow of $5,000, only the annual figures are different. For this and other reasons, these calculations are referred to as an indirect relationship between DCFR and return on net assets.

In Table 6–7, dividing the 5,000 by the BOY investments for the five years ($17,456) duplicates the 28.6%, which was the premise of the calculation. Note, however, that the sum of the BOY investments, $17,456, is greater than the sum of the average investments, shown in the return on assets calculation ($12,500). Herein lies the reason why a DCFR usually yields a lower return number than the same investment when calculated as a return on net assets.

With this explanation of the two different investment yardsticks, each of which is often called "rate of return," one can see that they should not be used interchangeably. Yet they often are. From this example, if you wish a return on net assets of 40% you need only require a DCFR of 28.6% from such investments to achieve that level of return on assets. Of course the numerical difference between the two return numbers varies with project life, but the general conclusion remains the same. A return on net assets is usually a larger number than a DCFR for the same investment.

TABLE 6-7
A Comparison of DCFR and RNA For Same Investment
(BFIT)

Return on Net Assets

	BOY Inv	Cash Inflow	Earnings (Profit)	Inv Rec	BOY Inv	Avg Inv
1	5,000	2,000	1,000	1,000	4,000	4,500
2	4,000	2,000	1,000	1,000	3,000	3,500
3	3,000	2,000	1,000	1,000	2,000	2,500
4	2,000	2,000	1,000	1,000	1,000	1,500
5	1,000	2,000	1,000	1,000	0	500
Total	15,000	10,000	5,000	5,000	10,000	12,500

$$\text{Return on Net Assets} = \frac{5,000}{12,500} = 40\%$$

Confirmation of DCFR Return

	BOY Inv	Cash Inflow	Earnings 28.6%	Inv Rec	EOY Inv
0	5,000				5,000
1	4,433	2,000	1,433	567	4,433
2	3,703	2,000	1,270	730	3,703
3	2,764	2,000	1,061	939	2,764
4	1,556	2,000	792	1,208	1,556
5		2,000	444	1,556	0
Total	17,456	10,000	5,000	5,000	17,456

$$\text{DCFR return} = \frac{5,000}{17,456} = 28.6\%$$

TABLE 6-8

	Actual Cash Flow, $	Earnings @28.6%, $
0	−5,000	—
1	2,000	1,433
2	2,000	1,270
3	2,000	1,061
4	2,000	792
5	2,000	444
Totals	5,000	5,000

Present Value Profit (PVP) and Inflation

Although we shall have more to say about inflation, one aspect of discounting should be noted. If the minimum guideline for your investments is 10% (as illustrated in this book), it probably assumes only small rates of inflation. Some analysts have raised the discount factor to include inflation, feeling this represents an adequate way of compensating for the loss in value of future dollars.

For example, if inflation is expected at 5% per year, then discounting the cash flows at 15% would include 10% for the minimum guideline and 5% for inflation. This method demonstrates one way to handle inflation. There are other ways to be covered in a more complete handling of inflation in a later chapter.

Changing the Point of Discounting

One final comment on discounting is needed. The examples shown in this chapter are for end-of-the-year discounting. We began our discussion of discounting by reviewing how money grows through compound interest. We discussed compounding at more frequent intervals than annually, but stated that in this book annual compounding was illustrated. Likewise, the discounting illustrated was for cash flow at the end of the year. Some existing computer programs used midyear discounting. Midyear discount factors produce, in all instances, less severe discounting and therefore higher present value profits for the same discount rate. For example, the 10% discount factors for year one and year two, using end-of-the-year discounting, are 0.909 and 0.826. The same factors for the same discount rate (10%), but using midyear discounting, are 0.953 and 0.867. The latter numbers are calculated using decimal midpoints. For year one the factor is derived from the fraction in which the numerator of one is divided by $(1 + i)$ raised to the 0.5 power. For year two the midyear factor is determined by dividing one by $(1 + i)$ to the 1.5 power. Because you get different present value profits from the two points of discounting, make sure that you know whether your computer program is using midyear, end-of-the-year or some other point of discounting. For example, using the midyear discount factors (10%) for the cash flows of the School prospect produces a present value of $2.402—6.6% higher than the end-of-the-year discounting of $2.254. Midyear and end-of-the-year discounting are the most popular.

REVIEW

Present value concepts are really time value concepts. The yardsticks available from present value relationships are reviewed in the next chapter. Nevertheless, we can already understand some of the importance of the time value of money.

Present value concepts are not difficult to use or understand if one remembers that money invested earns income called interest. In a profit-making organization, one must remember that the investor can always leave his money in the bank, at almost no risk, and get a small return. The profit-making organization which has risks of failure must achieve a return higher than a bank; otherwise it cannot attract new capital for investment.

BIBLIOGRAPHY

1. Kaitz, Melvin, "Percentage Gain on Investment—An Investment Decision Yardstick," *Journal of Petroleum Technology,* May 1967.
2. Arps, J.J, "Profitability Analysis of Proposed Capital Expenditures for Development Drilling and Appraisal of Producing Properties," AIME Petroleum Engineer Transactions, V. 213, 1958.
3. Hugo, G.R., "Farmouts Can Make Capital Efficient," *Oilweek,* Oct. 2, 1967.
4. Pollack, Gerald A., "The Capital Budgeting Controversy: Present Value vs Discounted Cash Flow Methods," NAA Bulletin, Nov. 1961, pg. 5.

5. Cotton, Frank E., "Investment Indicators for Profitability Analysis Must Reflect Recent Economic Developments," *Oil & Gas Journal*, Oct. 17, 1983, pp. 113-122.

PROBLEMS

1. If you invest $1,000 at 10%, how many years elapse before you have one million dollars? Clue: remember how many years it takes to double your money at 10% compounded annually. Use the Rule of 72.

2. Using a hand calculator and the discount factors in Table 6–3, combine the investment and income cash flows shown in Table 6–9. Calculate the actual value profit, payout and maximum negative cash flow. Then discount the annual cash flows at several discount rates to plot a present value profit and determine a DCFR.

TABLE 6-9
Calculating a DCFR

	Cash Flows - AFIT				Discounted Cash Flows		
	Invest	Inc.	Net	Cum	10%	20%	30%
0	-200	—					
1	-900	200					
2	-100	300					
3		400					
4		400					
5		300					
6		300					
7		200					
8		100					
9		100					
Total							

Payout = $\dfrac{\text{Maximum Negative Cash Flow}}{\rule{3cm}{0.4pt}}$ = _____

DCFR = _____

7 Measuring an Opportunity

As we start this chapter, let's review our progress to this point—we have made considerable progress.

1. We understand a few new terms needed for our investment evaluations.
2. We are aware of the significance of tax planning.
3. We can construct a cash flow stream.
4. We have a beginning understanding of the time value of money.

We now have sufficient knowledge to begin measuring our opportunities. We do this by comparing opportunities by means of investment yardsticks. This chapter will help us become acquainted with standard investment yardsticks.

Evolution of Investment Evaluation

For a change of pace, we are going to indulge in a bit of history—to show how we got to where we are in investment evaluation, and why.

Throughout the history of the oil industry, there has been a gradual evolution in investment policies, opportunities, and evaluations. Yardsticks have been developed with time to fit the state of knowledge, skill, technology and even political conditions. When one views the changes to date, future changes seem to be implied.

Pre-proration Era

In the pre-proration era, prior to 1930, the industry operated in an unstable economic climate. The instability was caused by numerous factors:

1. The ubiquitous cyclic nature of discoveries caused vast ranges in petroleum supplies from shortage to surplus.
2. Violent supply trends caused or abetted equally violent price trends.
3. Limited knowledge about fluid behavior in reservoirs, the geologic configuration of reservoirs, and the large numbers of individual operators conducting producing operations over bits and portions of an oil pool inhibited proper corrective measures.

Under such conditions of instability, the most important consideration for the producer was to get his money back quickly. How much it cost and the delay in return of capital were his prime yardsticks. Payout, or payback, became one of the first important yardsticks. Usually measured in years, payout is the time required for the opportunity to return the original investment. The shorter the time, the lower the risks.

The Beginning of Proration, 1930–1942

The primary concern of the regulatory agencies in establishing uniform measures of control was conservation. However, one of the byproducts of sound conservation was an era of stable prices. Producers could plan further ahead. The consumer also gained. He had assurances of a continuous stable supply for his energy needs.

For the producer price stability meant the ability to forecast future income for periods longer than a few months. He could estimate total future profit with more certainty. He could even borrow a little money on a good producing property. For the first time, the total quantity of money to be gained could be estimated with reasonable accuracy and the ratio of this amount to the original investment now had meaning. The profit-to-investment ratio could be considered an important economic yardstick. Two investments with identical payouts could be meaningfully compared on another basis, profit-to-investment ratio.

Reservoir engineering was born during this period. It also was a pertinent factor in enabling the producer to forecast his future income with greater accuracy.

In the pre-proration era and during the proration era (pre-1943), the cost of finding hydrocarbons was nominal. Discoveries were shallow, acreage cheap and there were lots of unexplored basins. Although the seismograph was introduced and the first formal exploration programs planned, yardsticks were, in most companies, applied only to exploitation investments. It was the development well and its related facilities which received the most economic scrutiny.

The War Years, 1943–1947

The war years produced a capacity production situation with sharply limited material supplies. Development of existing fields was given the highest priority and many attractive exploration investment opportunities lay dormant for lack of manpower and material. The scarcity of these two factors became more the limiting criteria than normal economic yardsticks. All activities had wartime priorities. Such materials as steel, transportation equipment, cement, etc. were allocated based on government established priorities.

Little change in investment evaluation occurred during this period.

From Capacity to Surplus, 1948–1957

After World War II the pent-up demand for hydrocarbons soared. Oil operators, still suffering from manpower and material shortages, strained to meet demands.

In 1948 a capacity situation existed for most of the year. For a time even Texas produced at its maximum efficient rate (often called MER). Spurred by the needs and with price responses, the petroleum industry undertook an extensive exploration and exploitation program. The program was so successful that between 1948 and 1962 the state of Texas, in response to an ever-increasing supply, reduced its market demand factor. This factor declined from 100% in 1948 to a low of about 26% in 1962.

There were other developments during this period. The rapid increase in demand brought upward changes in the price of crude oil and natural gas. The change was particularly significant for natural gas, long an underpriced energy source. Natural gas cannot be easily stored; and the cost of transporting it is about three times the cost of transporting an equivalent amount of BTUs in the form of crude oil. However, in terms of pollution, natural gas is the cleanest of all hydrocarbon fuels and in the switch to a period of surplus, it could be secured under long-term contracts favorable to the purchaser.

In the 1948–1957 period, natural gas prices at the wellhead increased at a faster rate than those of crude oil. As the price for natural gas increased, new reserves were developed from basins considered uneconomical at lower prices. The Arkoma basin of Oklahoma and Arkansas is a good example. Drilling is expensive in this hard rock country and known gas reserves could not be developed at a profit. About the time prices began to increase, the technology of drilling with air in hard rocks was introduced. The combination of increased price and air drilling made a previous unattractive basin a place for profitable exploration investments.

During the hectic days to supply an exploding demand for petroleum products, some operators forgot about interfuel competition. They assumed a future of continuous crude price increases. As a result many of the efficiencies later to be used were deferred by several years. They were introduced in the 1960s when costs were going up but prices were not.

The 1948–1957 period was characterized by rapidly increasing costs of finding hydrocarbons. There were few changes in evaluation criteria.

The Period of Surplus, 1957–1966

The best picture of surplus capacity is shown by Fig. 7–1. This figure plots a history of Texas proration. The market demand factor (%) is plotted from 1946 through 1977. A steady decrease in market demand factor followed the capacity period of 1948. The sharpest

Fig. 7–1 History of Texas proration, 1946–1977

drop came in 1958. The closing of the Suez Canal in 1957 had temporarily held demand at levels near those of the preceding years. After the Canal opened, the large surplus capacity in the U.S. forced Texas to prorate production to the lowest level in its history. The low point came in 1962 when the market demand factor was about 26%.

The industry has received much criticism, particularly from economists, because of its proration policies. The state of Texas has shared in this criticism. But Texas had several objectives in this matter and they were reasonable ones. The most important factors were conservation and protection of individual property rights. Each property owner was given his pro rata share of the market even though this market was restricted.

Another factor was revenue. The tax levied on petroleum and natural gas by the state is based on value. To see this value lowered by a temporary surplus would mean a permanent loss in revenue for Texas, something which the state leaders did not wish to happen. A few states have taxes unrelated to value. To protect its revenue for the citizens of Texas, to protect property rights, and to maintain proper conservation practices, severe proration was instituted. The spare capacity thus created was to be of considerable importance in the second closing of the Suez Canal.

The economic effect of severe proration is to limit production and revenue, lengthen payout and sharply restrict a company's ability to grow. We noted the reasons Texas was particularly hard hit by surplus capacity. Louisiana, whose tax is related to the barrel not value, also restricted production during this period. Again, the primary concern was conservation—to avoid physical and thus economic waste.

Severe proration resulted in a close scrutiny of all investments. Particular emphasis was placed on those investments that were capable of a high cash flow. The result was a growing appreciation of yardsticks associated with concepts of the time value of money. The present value profile, DCFR, and even accelerated income investments were considered. An accelerated income investment is one made primarily to obtain an advantage in timing of income. Often it implies for an oil property no increase in ultimate recovery, but greater recovery in the early years with reduced income in later years. Such investments can give a present value profit, but an actual value loss; e.g., going from 80- to 40-acre spacing would be an example of an accelerated income investment. If there were no increase in recovery, the extra investment would mean an actual value loss compared to 80-acre spacing—even though larger revenues early in the cash flow stream would yield a PVP.

As companies looked for larger cash flows, and optimum selections of investments and reviewed new concepts of risk evaluation, the resultant evolution in yardsticks was considerable. In addition, the advent of the computer significantly changed the number of alternates which could be reviewed in a short time.

The Surplus Ends, 1966-1970

Refer again to Fig. 7–1. The period of surplus crude ends after 1966. From that point on the proration factor increased sharply and reached 100% in April of 1972. Thus, the year 1973 represents the first year of essentially capacity production for the state of Texas. The state has been at capacity production ever since. There are individual fields which could produce at a slightly higher rate. These fields produce at MER rates deemed by the RRC to prevent waste. Excessive producing rates can, in certain reservoirs, result in lost production.

The trend in the market demand factor indicates the enhanced cash flow for the industry in the 1970s. This factor plus increased prices at the wellhead provided more funds which sought opportunities for reinvestment. As long as profitable opportunities exist in exploration, much of the cash flow will be reinvested in new prospects. When these opportunities diminish, the funds will seek investments in related energy fields. The purchase of coal and uranium reserves by a few oil companies indicates possible avenues for diversification. However, the sharp increases in rig use and seismic crews indicate a good climate for investments in the petroleum industry.

The Era of Regulation, after 1970

The full impact of bludgeoning regulation on yardstick evolution is unknown. The increased necessity of forecasting future prices, delay, permitting, etc., stretched the abilities of all analysts. The regulatory era had the same economic impact as severely restricted production—because in the end it resulted in lost income or delayed income. As a result, payouts lengthened, revenue was uncertain and startup dates became only approximate guesses unrelated to technical ability. The methods by which analysts coped with this era evolved. In numerous instances probabilities of occurrence were assigned to factors once considered relatively fixed.

The results of the regulatory era were investment evaluations and forecasts with a new element of uncertainty. Forecasts of income from existing fields took on new uncertainties as rules and regulations (for wellhead prices, safety regulations, stringent specifications for drilling in the OCS, etc.) changed. Historically, investments suffer if the investment climate bodes increased uncertainty. Nevertheless, as we shall see, yardsticks to review investment opportunities evolve to cope with new situations.

The Unprecedented Boom and Its Collapse, 1979–1987

The regulatory period was followed by a modest softening of some kinds of rules and regulations. Crude prices were deregulated and provisions were made through the Natural Gas Policy Act to deregulate most gas supplies in the mid-1980s. The Windfall Profit Tax remained during this period.

The regulatory period was followed by the most unusual period in the history of the petroleum industry. The OPEC nations decided to drive prices up sharply. There was over a tenfold increase in the prices of crude oil in the decade prior to 1981—a totally unprecedented event. The high prices were sustained for a few years; but as individuals learned new methods of conservation, demand was reduced sharply. Portions of that demand decrease are permanent. Automobiles with more efficient engines and fewer pounds of weight consume less gasoline. Houses with new insulation will use fewer BTUs from now on; permanent changes in energy usage occurred with the price increases.

Fig. 7–2 shows the prices of crude oil and natural gas at the wellhead for the U.S. from 1946 through 1987. Because of the unusually high prices of the early 1980s, the earlier eras seem almost stable. The average U.S. price reached almost $32 per barrel in 1981 and began its collapse from that point. By 1987 wellhead crude prices averaged about $16 per barrel, having bounced back from the low of $12.66 per barrel in 1986. Never before had the petroleum industry had such sharp increases in revenue followed by sustained collapse. The price decline from 1981 through 1986 was among the longest in industry's history.

The price graph shows a little about the history of each of the eras. Changing price levels for natural gas and crude oil are shown. Through most of the period, natural gas prices increased faster than those for crude oil, as this cheap fuel approached its competitive BTU value. On a strictly BTU basis, it takes about 6 Mcf to equal one barrel of crude oil. Throughout most of the periods shown in Fig. 7–2, you

Fig. 7–2 U.S. average wellhead prices

could get from 20 to 25 Mcf for the same price as a barrel of crude oil. The scale on the graph for natural gas shows a ten-to-one relationship. Thus, if the gas curve is on the same level as the oil curve, the value relationship is ten Mcf per barrel, not the six Mcf per barrel indicated by the inherent BTU comparison. Natural gas prices approached the ten-to-one relationship and actually were below ten-to-one in the years 1983–1986. They appear, however, to be headed toward the ten-to-one or more in the later years of the 1980s.

Fig. 7–3 shows that even though prices appear to change little over time, on a percentage basis historically they have varied considerably. On this graph, crude price changes are plotted as a function of the percent change from the prior year. In the early 1980s there were five successive years of price decreases, the worst being over 40% in 1986. Only twice since 1914 has such a large decrease occurred. Price volatility has been the history of the petroleum industry!

In the boom-collapse period, yardsticks were still evolving. New concepts emerged to handle problems perceived with existing yard-

Fig. 7–3   Crude price changes at wellhead

sticks. There was a renewed emphasis on enhancing corporate wealth and new ideas as to how this should be measured. Yardsticks evolve to meet the situations of the time.

Investment Yardsticks

Now back to measuring an opportunity. First let's review the term investment. In investment evaluation any expenditure made in the expectation of an increased profit can be regarded as an investment. (We usually look at the after-tax expenditures as we saw in Chapter 5.) Contrast this concept with the accounting definition where the investment refers only to those expenditures which are capitalized. Therefore, investment evaluation implies:

1. The expectation of future profits, usually involving both uncertainty and risk.
2. Income generated over a period of time.
3. A freedom of choice among investments, i.e., the discretion to select the best from various opportunities.

Investment yardsticks are the various criteria we use to help us in measuring, comparing and describing investment opportunities. In this chapter we will define most of the commonly used yardsticks and illustrate the use of yardsticks with example cases.

The Ideal Yardstick

It would be extremely useful if there were a single yardstick which properly ranked each investment opportunity. We would probably call this measurement the ideal yardstick. It would have certain characteristics.

1. It would illustrate the effect on corporate profits of making a specific investment.
2. It would isolate only those investment opportunities which are acceptable to established guidelines.
3. It would always make the proper choice from a group of mutually exclusive opportunities. (In a group of investment opportunities, if only one may finally be selected, the investments are said to be mutually exclusive.)

Unfortunately, no ideal yardstick exists. As a result, several yardsticks are necessary for proper evaluation of an opportunity. Wise decisions are more likely when measuring an opportunity from several viewpoints. Some yardsticks require special care. They may be constructed differently by different individuals. When using any yardstick, be sure you understand how it was calculated. Was it before tax or after tax; booked investment or after-tax expenditures; present or actual value?

A few opportunities are good investments almost by inspection; but very large investments, marginal investments, or high-risk investments demand more careful scrutiny. Investments in areas unfamiliar to management (new geology or new industry) also require more evaluation. It is the bane of the investment analyst that his requester usually wants one more yardstick than those calculated—and that he spends a disproportionate amount of time evaluating marginal investments.

Common Investment Yardsticks

Yardsticks from cash flow analysis. From Chapter 5 we learned that several useful factors are developed from cash flow analysis. Cash flow techniques directly provide many common yard-sticks and are the basis for others. The yardsticks from cash flow analysis are:

1. The investment—both before and after tax. It may be separated into exploratory investments and producing investments. These are sometimes expressed on a unit basis (i.e., $/bbl.). If so, the before tax expenditure is used.
2. Maximum negative cash flow. The largest sum of money, out-of-pocket at any one time, is called the maximum negative cash flow. You calculated this in the problem at the end of Chapter 5.
3. Ultimate net profit or loss. The cumulative net cash flow from a project is its ultimate net income (or profit). It is the sum of inflows minus outflows and is often called the actual value profit (AVP).
4. Ultimate net income ratio. The total actual value profit divided by the cumulative maximum negative cash flow is called the ultimate net income ratio.
5. Profit-to-investment ratio. The total actual value profit divided by investment is the profit-to-investment ratio. Please note that the term investment has not been defined. Be sure when you see a profit-to-investment ratio (P:I or P/I) that you understand just what investment is being used. Is it before tax or after tax? Originally, this yardstick was used only with the capitalized investment. Use this yardstick with care and always define your investment.

Yardsticks that reflect timing.   Certain yardsticks are related to time. Some have a calendar significance and others reflect the time value of money.

1. Project life. The length of a project in years is the project life. This yardstick has significance for a corporation. Its importance is related to a corporation's view of the future. Inflation, changing taxes, variable risks, changing energy patterns, etc. can encourage a company to favor either long or short project life depending on its goals.
2. Payout period. The time in years to return the after-tax investment is called payout. The payout is calculated from the net cash flow stream. The point at which the cumulative net cash flow becomes positive is the project's payout.

3. Present value profit. A discounted net cash flow stream is called a present value profit—or if negative, a present value loss. It must always be expressed with an accompanying percentage which tells you the discount factor used to reduce the cash flow. Present value profits are usually shown at commonly quoted discount rates (10% for example).

4. Present value profile. The curve resulting from plotting present value profits versus their discount rates is called the present value profile. We shall review this yardstick in much more detail. Its configuration is important in investment evaluation.[1]

5. Discounted cash flow rate. (Sometimes called investor's interest rate.) The discount per cent which reduces a cash flow stream to zero is called the discounted cash flow rate.

6. Discounted profit-to-investment ratio. This yardstick measures investment efficiency. Given two projects with equal discounted profits, choose the one with the smallest investment. Sometimes this yardstick is written: PVP @ HR divided by I where: PVP is the present value profit, HR is the hurdle rate or the minimum acceptable rate of return and I is the investment, which is also discounted if the investment stream goes beyond year zero.

The comment related to I, above, is important. When using, or reviewing this yardstick, take care to assure that the investment has been discounted. A common mistake in using this yardstick is to forget that I too must be discounted if investments are made in other than year zero.

Yardsticks based on accounting concepts.

1. Booked investment. Those items which would be capitalized on the corporate books make up booked investment.

2. Annual, cumulative and average booked net income. The net profit (or loss) reported to stockholders is the booked net income.

3. Annual or average booked rate of return. The booked net income divided by the average net booked investment is the booked rate of return. It is often called the return on net assets. It can be shown for a single year, cumulative to some point in time, or an average over project life.

Yardsticks related to risk. So far we haven't mentioned risk. Chapters nine and ten dwell on this subject. Risk may or may not be taken into account in calculating project economics. It is handled in different ways, depending upon the type of risk and the degree of risk.

1. Some risks are weighted for evaluation. We shall review risk weighting.
2. Other risks are not enumerated but are covered in an evaluation by a qualifying statement.
3. Risks are sometimes handled by yanking the minimum criteria high enough to offset (hopefully) the unknown risk. Raising the minimum investment criteria is often done; commonly, it is an increase in the minimum DCFR. Such an increase is, however, a less desirable correction than that of re-evaluating the assumptions (projections, etc.) for the analysis, particularly those that caused sufficient concern to require a higher DCFR. For example, foreign investments (particularly those in countries with unstable governments) require higher DCFR, if that is the method of correction. Another way to handle this dilemma is to raise the risk factor (political risk factor) and leave the minimum DCFR the same. The advantage of raising the political risk factor is that it focuses on the particular factor causing concern. It provides a more logical basis to evaluate the investment and for comparison to other investments. After all, the critical factor is political risk. Why not show that directly and not raise the minimum DCFR to some arbitrary level?
4. The interrelation of numerous risks is evaluated by a mathematical technique often referred to as Monte Carlo simulation. It sums randomly the probabilities of each event occurring and produces a probability distribution for the combined risks. A computer is needed for this treatment of risks.

Investment Yardsticks and the School Prospect

We have now discussed yardsticks and it is time to see them in application. We shall use the School prospect to review our knowledge of yardsticks.

Yardsticks Related to Cash Flow

First, let's review the total expenditures before and after tax. They were:

	$M	
	Total	**AFIT**
Investment	6,200	4,792
Exploration expenditures	3,000	2,323
Development expenditures	3,200	2,469

Note that the AFIT investment is shown as $4,792,000. This number is used in cash flow analysis. The capitalized investment was less—$3.6 million.

These expenditures are used with other data to construct additional yardsticks. The net cash flow or actual value profit (AVP) was $6.988 million, the same as the total booked net income (corporate profit). To get a profit-to-investment ratio for the School prospect, all we do is divide the total net profit (net cash flow) by the investment. The net profit used is always the AVP (in total), but what investment do you use? The total investment? The capitalized investment? The after-tax investment? Let's compare these for the School prospect.

Profit-to-Investment Ratios	P/I
Based on total expenditures:	$\frac{6.998}{6.200} = 1.13$
Based on AFIT investment:	$\frac{6.998}{4.792} = 1.46$
Based on capitalized investment:	$\frac{6.998}{3.600} = 1.94$

Forty years ago the net profit was most frequently related to the capitalized investment. It is seldom related to before-tax expenditures. Cash flow analysis has introduced a new term, however, the *ultimate net income ratio* (UNIR). Here the total net profit, ultimate net income, is related to the maximum negative cash flow; e.g., in the School prospect the ultimate net income ratio is:

$$\text{UNIR} = \frac{6.998}{2.616} = 2.68$$

Whenever the maximum negative cash flow is smaller than the after-tax investment or the capitalized investment, the ultimate net income rate will be higher than the other profit-to-investment ratios. In general, this condition is true more often than not; therefore, the UNIR is usually larger than most commonly used P/I ratios.

Yardsticks Related to Timing

Next let's examine yardsticks related to timing for the School prospect.

Project life—years	13
Payout period—years	6.0
Discounted cash flow rate—%	24.5
From the PV profile—	
PV profit ($M) @ 10%	2,254
PV profit ($M) @ 20%	436
PV profit ($M) @ 30%	−340

Yardsticks Related to Accounting Procedures

Although not used extensively in investment analysis, it is advisable to understand those yardsticks related to accounting procedures. For the School prospect these are:

Capitalized investment—$M	3,600
Booked rate of return—%	46.7
Total booked net income—$M	6,998

A Comparison of Investments

With all these yardsticks how do you sort the "wheat from the chaff?" Remember we said there is no ideal yardstick; but what are the important ones? We can best answer this question by a comparison of three investments. Such a comparison is shown in the following table.

TABLE 7–1

Comparison of Investment Yardsticks

Yardstick	Opportunity		
	A	B	C
Investment, after FIT* $	300	300	300
Actual value profit $	1,650	1,140	300
Project life-years	35	15	2
Ultimate net income ratio	5.5	3.8	1.0
PV profit, discounted @ 10% $	300	405	222
Payout-years	5.0	3.3	1.0
DCF rate (IIR) %	21	35	58
Booked return %	75	60	50

* Maximum negative cash flow in this example.

In Table 7–1 we compare three investment opportunities, each with different income characteristics but with an identical investment of $300. Investment A has the largest AVP of $1,650. By this standard it is the best. Investment C has the shortest project life. You get your money back quickly also with its 1.0 year payout. A, however, has the highest UNIR, but B has the largest PVP at 10%. C has the largest DCFR of 58%, but A has the biggest booked return of 75%. Thus, each investment has one or more yardsticks where it exceeds the others. Which is the best investment?

There is no clear cut answer to this question. We must know other related facts. For example, what are corporate objectives? If the corporation wants any investment to make a DCFR of 20% or more then all three qualify. If the company is not capital limited, it makes all three investments. Suppose it can make only one. Which one would you make? Again, it depends on another factor. If you could make C first and still take advantage of A or B one year later, that would be the best route because of C's fast payout. If you can only make one and the other two won't be available in one year, then you must choose between A and B since they give greater profits for a single investment.

If you don't have a lot of alternate investments and want the most AVP for the investment, take A; but B is better if you will have another 30% opportunity before the end of five years.

We haven't mentioned risk. Before a final decision could be made, you must consider the element of risk.

Comparisons Using Present Value Yardsticks

One can use the shape of a PV profile to help understand a single investment and to compare two or more investments.

Fig. 7–4 is such a comparison. A few additional yardsticks are shown for each prospect on the right hand side.

Prospect A is obviously a long-life project and it has the highest AVP of $8,500,000. Prospect B has a shorter life and a lower AVP but higher discounted profits than A at 8, 10, and 20%. Similar, now familiar, characteristics for the School prospect are also shown.

Here is what Fig. 7–4 tells us if we use only PV concepts as our investment criteria:

1. Assuming no risk and a minimum guideline no lower than 10% DCFR, all are good investments.
2. At discount rates below 5%, prospect A is the best.

Fig. 7–4   Three prospects with different investments and cash flow
streams

3. At discount rates between 5% and 17.5%, the School prospect
   is the best investment.
4. If you have alternate investments with DCFRs greater than
   17.5%, then prospect B is the best investment.

We must consider more than PV concepts; nevertheless, they add
to our storehouse of information about a prospect.

Growth Rate—A New Yardstick

Yardsticks are subject to revision and new ones are being added
each year. In fact, a continuous search for better yardsticks goes on all
the time. The search results from the desire to improve upon the
weaknesses of existing yardsticks.

One example of this search is the yardstick called "Growth Rate."
As documented by Capen, et. al[2], it is a measure of investment
efficiency. It can be expressed as future dollars or as a rate of return.
The principal objective of growth rate is to answer an objection to
DCFR. A high DCFR usually is well above a company's average return

on investment. Therefore, cash flows received in future years cannot really be reinvested at the high rate indicated by the DCFR.

Growth rate attempts to answer this flaw by saying in effect "why not invest all future positive cash flows at the average company return?" This solution uses the "real world" rate of return and measures the growth of future cash flows to some future target year.

As a measure of investment efficiency, growth rate can be expressed as the present worth per dollar invested. However, this expression introduces yet another PW/I ratio to a host of such ratios and a percentage, if meaningful, can be grasped more quickly. For this reason a growth rate of return can be calculated, yielding a percentage as the final answer. If you are uncertain as to which yardstick answer would be the most easily understood, supply the requestor with the PW/I ratio and the percentage.

Calculating Growth Rate of Return

How does one calculate this yardstick? The growth rate of return (GRR) is calculated by the following steps:

Step   **Action**
1 Compound (at the average company reinvestment rate) all positive cash flows forward to some target year (t).
2 Positive cash flows beyond the target year are discounted back to the target year.
3 Negative cash flows are discounted to the present at the same rate used in step one. The sum of the discounted negative cash flows is considered the investment (I).
4 The sum of the cash flows in steps one and two is designated as B.
5 Calculate the GRR as follows:

$$\text{GRR} = \left(\frac{B}{I}\right)^{\frac{1}{t}} - 1$$

where:

GRR = the growth rate of return (multiply the decimal answer by 100 to get a percent)

B = the sum of positive compounded cash flows to time t (target year) and the discounted cash flows beyond t

t = target year

I = the sum of the negative cash flows discounted to year zero.

Examples of GRR Combinations

The various combinations of factors influencing growth rate are demonstrated in Table 7–2. In column one is the net cash flow stream for the School prospect. It totals $6.998 million but is composed of a negative stream of $2.661 million and a positive stream of $9.614 million.

Columns 3, 4 and 5 show the cash flows developed when three different target years are used. Keep in mind that column one is the actual net cash flow. The other columns are created based on different assumptions of compounding (to the target year) and discounting (annual flows beyond the target year). The cash flow in column two has been compounded and discounted appropriately as outlined in the first four steps of the GRR calculation. For simplicity, annual compounding was assumed and the annual cash flow was assumed to have been received at yearend. The reinvestment rate used was 10%.

In column three, the target year (t) was eight and the resultant calculation of the GRR was:

$$GRR_{10} = \left(\frac{9509}{2158}\right)^{1/8} - 1 = 20.4\%$$

Column four, with t = 10, produces a GRR of 18.2% and column five at t = 13 has a GRR of 16.3%. Varying the target year makes a difference. However, according to Capen, et. al, the relative relationship between investments will not be altered by a change in t; therefore, it does not lose its discriminatory value.

In columns 3, 4 and 5, the discounted value of negative cash flows was used in the investment. Just for comparison, column 2 shows the positive cash flows compounded to t = 8, but with the negative cash flows not discounted. In this case:

$$GRR_{10} = \left(\frac{9509}{2616}\right)^{1/8} - 1 = 17.5\%$$

TABLE 7-2
Various Calculations of Growth Rate
School Prospect, $M

	1	2	3	4	5
	Net Cash Flow		Growth Rate @ 10%		
		I = 2616	I = 2158		
Year		t = 8	t = 8	t = 10	t = 13
0	-500	-500	-500	-500	-500
1	-232	-232	-211	-211	-211
2	-792	-792	-655	-655	-655
3	-799	-799	-600	-600	-600
4	-293	-293	-192	-192	-192
5	954	1270	1270	1536	2045
6	1622	1963	1963	2375	3161
7	1605	1765	1765	2136	2843
8	1593	1593	1593	1927	2566
9	783	712	712	861	1146
10	783	647	647	783	1042
11	768	577	577	698	929
12	753	514	514	622	828
13	753	468	468	565	753
Totals	6998	6893	7351	9345	13,155
B =	—	9509	9509	11,503	15,313

In other yardsticks in this chapter, "I" was never less than the maximum negative cash flow. The GRR, using the maximum negative cash flow, was calculated merely for comparison purposes and is not recommended. According to all cash flow theory and the theory of discounting, all investments (in this case the negative cash flows) should be discounted to year zero. We assume that future investment money is at work earning interest until needed.

The general theory behind the GRR is to pick a target year and see which investments accumulate the largest pile of money. To do this, money returned is compounded at the reinvestment rate out to the target year. The target year is the year of reference. It is for this reason that annual cash flows beyond the target year are discounted back to the target year. In a sense, the discounted cash flows are a rough estimate of what the property would sell for at the target year—which represents part of the pile of money.

What have we learned from the calculations in Table 7-2? It is obvious that GRR increases, at a constant I, as t becomes smaller. Capen, et. al demonstrated that GRR does increase as t approaches 0. As t increases, GRR decreases and approaches the reinvestment rate.

For the School prospect this relationship is confirmed in Fig. 7–5. A target year should begin beyond the last annual negative cash flow. Then, for the School prospect, t can be as small as five. The thirteenth year is the last positive cash flow year and can also be a target year. The plot in Fig. 7–5 demonstrates the range of GRR from t = 5 to t = 13. The GRR, expressed as a percent, varies from 27.1% at t = 5 to 16.3% at t = 13. So it is possible to have GRR values both above and below the DCFR value of 24.5%. At a target year of 6 or 7, the GRR is close to the DCFR value.

Advantages of GRR

Since certain groups are using this yardstick preferentially, they must consider it to have advantages. What are these advantages?

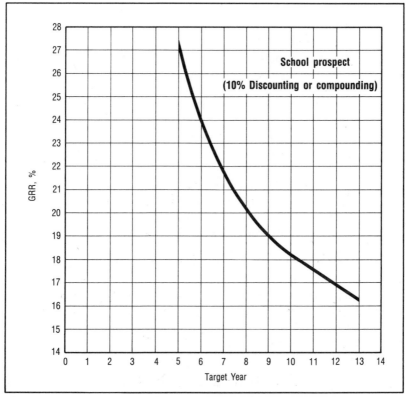

Fig. 7–5   Growth rate of return varies with target year

1. Growth rate is not a trial-and-error process as is DCFR. Therefore the calculations are easier.
2. Growth rate shows what the company can expect if the future cash flows are reinvested at its average rate of return.
3. Growth rate of return is an extension of present worth per dollar invested. It produces a percentage for those accustomed to a percentage to compare investments.

Are There Disadvantages?

Although they might not qualify as severe disadvantages, several key decisions must be made relative to GRR.

1. The choice of the time horizon (t) must be made. The final choice won't change project ranking by GRR, so what target year should you use? Probably you should use one which produces percentages close to those normally seen by your management.
2. The reinvestment rate must be chosen. The problems here stem from varying functional rates of return. If your function consistently outperforms the other functions of the company, the average company reinvestment rate may be below what you should be using. Some companies have functions for which no reinvestment rate is calculated. In these cases, a borrowing rate might be used. Whatever the difficulties, a decision must be made on the reinvestment rate.
3. The definition of investment must be considered. There should be few problems with the recommendation of Capen et. al to use the discounted negative cash flows as I. Nevertheless, this I is less than almost all other concepts of investment.

The extended discussion of growth rate and GRR illustrates the search for more definitive yardsticks. For exploration investments one should make sure that risk and risk alone does not swamp all minor differences in yardstick percentages. Our risks are still primarily geological ones. This observation should in no way detract from the search for more meaningful yardsticks.

Other Evaluations

We began this section by stating that yardsticks can be revised. Several new innovations result from the modifications of existing, long-used yardsticks.

An interesting modification of payout was proposed by Robert A. Campbell and J.M. Campbell, Jr.[3] It is discounted payout. The logic behind the change is to require the investment to return not only the principal but also the interest required to make the investment.

Campbell and Campbell also list other new yardsticks which are being tested. Most incorporate the discounted payout (DPO) as part of the yardstick. A brief description of these yardsticks follows:

Treasury worth (TW)—TW is computed as the discounted cash flow before DPO plus the undiscounted cash flow after DPO.

Treasury worth index (TWI)—An index of the discounted cash flow before DPO plus undiscounted cash flow after payout (TW) divided by the investment.

Accrued treasury assets (ATA)—ATA is the sum of discounted cash flow until DPO, plus the accrued value of all cash flows after DPO. ATA differs from TW in that it develops an equivalent future value after payout. In contrast, TW develops an equivalent present value.

Treasury growth rate (TGR)—This yardstick utilizes the ATA concept to develop a rate of return. To calculate TGR you compound all cash flows after DPO, then discount all cash flows prior to DPO. Campbell and Campbell show the relationship between ATA and TGR as follows:

$$I \, (1 \, + \, TGR)^n \, = \, ATA$$

where n is the year of the last cash flow—the end of the project.

Modified Internal Rate of Return

We discussed the reinvestment assumptions inherent in DCFR (IRR) calculations in the previous chapter. To some analysts these assumptions limit the usefulness of the DCFR as a yardstick. Also, each change in sign can produce another DCFR value. Multiple answers are confusing to say the least and the modified internal rate of return (MIRR) avoids the multiple answers. In the MIRR negative cash flows are discounted at a rate that reflects the return on a fully liquid investment (bond, CD, etc.) Positive cash flows are reinvested at a rate that reflects the return on investments of comparable risk. The MIRR is somewhat akin to the Growth Rate of Return.

In summary, we see that TW is related to TWI in much the same manner as ATA is related to TGR. For comparing investments TGR can be given a common reference point (n) for a more equitable accept/reject criterion.

What Are The Best Yardsticks?

With the complete range of yardsticks available to us, what are the ones to use? As we have seen, this question is not answered easily. Let's relate our answer to the plight of the explorer. We shall use his perspective and emphasize the yardsticks that have the greatest value to him.

To begin, any exploratory investment must have a full documentation of risk and how it is handled. If your company has standardized risk methodology, fine. If it does not, a careful review of the risk consideration is in order, particularly how they are placed into the cash flow calculations. Risk is often not regarded as a yardstick, per se, yet it influences all calculations to a marked degree and must be reviewed for each exploratory opportunity.

Any analyst must consider other important aspects of the investment opportunity. The investment itself is important, as we saw in the consideration of discounted present value divided by the investment. The total quantity of money, both discounted and undiscounted, is of value for the corporation. The undiscounted value (AVP) represents tomorrow's net cash generation—vital to a corporation wanting to maintain its cash flow for dividends and future investments. Discounted profit-to-investment ratios are important. For the School prospect the PVP at 10% divided by the discounted I is 1.03, less than any of the other P/I ratios, yet useful because it measures investment efficiency.

The yardsticks chosen will be those with the most meaning to the decision makers. Managements with pipeline, insurance or utility backgrounds will often think in terms of return on investment, return on equity or return on capital employed, even though these measures are not appropriate discriminators for exploratory investments.

For the best yardsticks to make the right investment choices, those which more perfectly and consistently chose the best investments for company growth, the analyst should help his management move toward present value concepts where possible. Keeping in mind that a large company needs large investment opportunities to continue its growth, the GRR, discounted profit to investment, AFIT investment and total net cash flow are useful, important yardsticks. And don't forget the risk. It often overwhelms other aspects of the investment opportunity. In other words, the geology upon which an investment is based is *the* most important factor and we shall discuss its role in subsequent chapters. In the meantime, given an adequate geological background, chapter seven has introduced the full range of yardsticks used to select the best investments. Even with the greater risks of exploratory investments, these yardsticks are helpful in picking the right opportunities.

Yardsticks are changing and will change as new conditions emerge. We should expect change and be willing to test new concepts in measuring one investment relative to another.

REVIEW

There are related factors, beyond yardsticks alone, that must be considered to choose the right investment. They include:

1. Risk
2. Corporate objectives
3. Number of available opportunities
4. Available capital

Despite these limitations you can see that the various yardsticks tell you much of what you need to know about an investment opportunity. They do not make the decision, but they greatly assist the decision-maker.

The explorationist probably has more independent factors to consider than any other investment maker. His experience and judgment are vital to proper choices. Investment analysis can be one of his greatest tools and it will show him the economic consequences of his geologic assumptions.

BIBLIOGRAPHY

1. Wooddy, L.D., and Capshaw, T.D., "Investment Evaluation by Present Value Profile." Paper presented to the SPE annual meeting, Oct. 1959.
2. Capen, E.C., Clapp, R.V., and Phelps, W.W., "Growth Rate—A Rate of Return Measure of Investment Efficiency," *Journal of Petroleum Technology,* May 1976, pg. 531.
3. Campbell, Robert A., and Campbell, J.M., Jr., "Optimizing Treasury Growth With Proper Evaluation of Long Term Projects." Paper presented at SPE Meeting, Feb. 1977.

SUGGESTED READING

1. Ricks, Richard L., "Acquisition of Information—Economic Considerations," *Oil & Gas Journal*, Sept. 30, 1985, pg. 68.
2. "Evaluating & Managing Risk—A Collection of Readings," edited by Robert E. Megill, PennWell Books, Tulsa, Oklahoma, 1985, 152 pages.
3. Starks, Laura. "Economic Performance of Oil Projects Evaluated by Modified IRR," *Oil & Gas Journal*, April 22, 1985, pg. 71.

PROBLEMS

1. Take the net cash flow for the School prospect (Table 5–5) and remove the exploratory expenditures—years zero through three. Recalculate the DCFR for the truncated net cash flow. It represents the average DCFR for the development wells drilled on the School prospect.

Questions:
1. What is the DCFR for development wells?
2. Shown as a multiple, how much larger is the development DCFR than the DCFR for the entire prospect (including exploratory costs)?

2. Investment Yardsticks
Using the cash flow streams shown on the next page, determine the following:

  a. Actual Value Profit:
  b. Payout Period:
  c. Ultimate Net Income Ratio:
  d. Profit-to-BFIT Investment Ratio:
  e. 14% PVP/AFIT I (Net Effective) Ratio:
  f. Knowing that the 14%, 20% and 30% PVP values are $370M, $183M and −$42M respectively, plot a present value profile and determine the Discounted Cash Flow Rate.

3. Investment Yardsticks
As a manager of an independent oil company, you must decide which projects are profitable and compatible with company goals and objectives. Your diligent technical staff has evaluated and submitted the projects shown on page 132 for your approval.

Year	BFIT Investment	AFIT Investment	AFIT Cash Inflow	AFIT Net Cash Flow
0	900	530	0	(530) ⎫ (640)
1	500	460	350	(110) ⎭
2			250	250
3			290	290
4			270	270
5			260	260
6			250	250
7			210	210
8			180	180
9			160	160
10			80	80
Total:	1,400	990	2,300	1,310

List the project(s) which would be optimum or acceptable under the following conditions. (Assume your company's cost of capital is 10% and you have no other investment opportunities unless otherwise noted):

a. Capital limited to a total $6000M investment budget.

   Projects: Investment =   10% PVP =

b. Capital limited to a total of $3500M, your cost of capital is 15%, and Project T must be withdrawn because of political issues.

   Projects: / Investment =   15% PVP =

c. No limit on capital resources but your cost of capital is 10%.

d. Your spouse (51% owner of the company) issues an edict that no projects having a 10% PVP/AFIT investment ratio less than 0.35 can be initiated.

e. You have only projects T & U which are mutually exclusive. You are capital limited with other reinvestment opportunities having a PVP/I ratio equal to:

   (a) 0.5   (b) 0.35   (c) 0.25

What if T & U were not mutually exclusive? (a), (b), (c), conditions above.

AFIT NET CASH FLOW, $ M

Year	B	U	Y	I	T	N	O	W
0*	-1000	-1000	-1000	-1000	-500	-1000	-1000	-500
1	600	700	210	10	0	0	900	0
2	400	500	210	20	10	0	200	0
3	300	200	210	50	15	100	100	25
4	200	100	210	100	25	100	50	25
5	50	50	210	200	50	100	50	50
6	20	10	210	300	150	300	10	150
7	10	10	210	400	250	500	10	250
8	10	10	210	500	350	500	10	350
9	5	10	210	500	350	500	0	350
10	5	10	210	400	350	500	0	250

Investment Yardsticks

	B	U	Y	I	T	N	O	W
Payout (Yr.)	2.0	1.6	4.8	6.8	7.0	6.8	1.5	7.0
AVP/ Invest.	0.6	0.6	1.1	1.5	2.0	1.6	0.3	1.9
DCFR - %	25	28.5	16.5	13.4	15.0	13.8	20.0	14.7
AVP - $ M	600	600	1100	1480	1050	1600	330	950
5% PVP - $ M	432	448	622	724	518	794	227	487
10% PVP - $ M	294	323	290	230	208	270	139	188
15% PVP - $ M	179	217	54	-102	3	-81	64	-10

*BFIT Inv. = AFIT Inv.

f. Your budget is cut to $1000M and your cost of capital is

   (a) 5%   (b) 10%   (c) 15%

g. You decide to rank the projects in order of liquidity and take the four most attractive. (Payout is considered a measure of liquidity.)

8 The Minimum Rate of Return

Conditions change in any industry from time to time. But even in stable times a perennial question seems to be "What should be the minimum rate of return?" What is the absolute minimum below which the company should not invest? It is obvious that the minimum rate of return is related to the cost of capital. If your company has 60% equity and 40% debt, then the cost of borrowed capital carries a 40% weight and the dividend rate is weighted at 60% to derive the cost of capital. As we shall see later, rates of return for exploratory investments are often related to factors other than the cost of capital.

To understand what the minimum should be requires a comprehension of what the investment return is, how it is calculated and how this return is related to the expected minimum. The background in Chapters 6 and 7 will serve us well as we investigate the minimum rate of return (MROR).

The Minimum Rate and The DCFR

Not all companies use the same yardsticks to determine the minimum rate of return. The discounted cash flow rate (DCFR) is one of the most popular measures. It is often used as a screen to sort out those opportunities above a certain minimum. It is not the same number as the return on assets, as we saw in Chapter 7. It differs from a return on capital employed and a return on equity capital, both of which are much more related to return on assets.

The Minimum Rate and Return on Net Assets

From our example in Chapter 7, the DCFR for the School prospect was 24.5% and the return on net assets for the same prospect was

46.7%. For most cash flow streams, the DCFR will be smaller than the return on assets. So, the first step in establishing a minimum rate of return (hurdle rate) is to decide which base will be the one employed. For exploratory investments most companies use a minimum return guideline that is related to present value concepts (DCFR, GRR, etc.). Needless to say, a great deal of confusion can be created if management asks for a return on one basis, thinking it is another. Asking for a MROR of 15%, thinking of it as a return on assets—because that is what you now report to stockholders, is not the same as asking for a MROR on a DCFR basis.

Another important factor related to the return on assets is that it is sensitive to the amount of reinvestment. If a company has the good fortune to have many attractive investment opportunities, it may borrow money to make all of these investments. The individual prospects or investment opportunities may each be well above the minimum, but for the company as a whole, the report to stockholders for the next few years might show a lowering of the return on assets because of the heavy reinvestment rate. Remember, new investments are cash drains in the beginning; they have negative cash flows and thus negative returns on assets. So even if the MROR is related to recent company experience (on net assets), events can change the perspective of what the return will do in the future. Reducing reinvestment sharply raises the return on net assets for a company, because it is, in reality, liquidating. All of these considerations complicate the setting of a minimum rate of return (or hurdle rate).

Prospect vs. Development Well DCFR

There is another factor. One should not use the same rate of return for a development well as for an exploratory prospect. Just why this is so is easily shown by the following cash flow stream in Table 8–1.

The two cash flow streams are identical, except for the first two entries. Years zero and one represent the years of exploratory expenditures. Thus, for the column headed "prospect" the cash flow represents the entire expenditure and revenue flow from the beginning of exploratory activity. In the second column the years zero and one are omitted, i.e., the exploratory expenditures are removed so that we can look at the DCFR for the development wells only, which are represented by the stream beginning in year two. In any cash flow analysis for a prospect, removing the exploratory risks, timing and funds leaves a cash flow stream which is the return on the development wells for the prospect.

TABLE 8-1

Year	NCF—Prospect	NCF—Development Only
0	−500	—
1	−700	—
2	−1000	−1000
3	1000	1000
4	1000	1000
5	1000	1000
6	900	900
7	800	800
8	700	700
9	600	600
10	500	500
Total	4300	5500

Discounting the prospect cash flow stream yields a DCFR of 28.8%. Discounting the second column, with exploratory expenditures removed, the DCFR is 97.5%. Here we see the sharp difference between the cash flow stream for a prospect and a development well. The development well stream has no charges for "finding" the prospect. Returns on development wells must be at least two or three times that of a prospect. Otherwise, you are making no provision for future exploration. Again, the analogy of the grocer is proper. Selling goods from the shelves (drilling development wells) produces very high returns, but it does not take into account the purchase of stock (finding) for the shelves. The overall return for the grocery store must take into account the cost of restocking the shelves.

The MROR set for a prospect is a different level from that of a development well. The development well MROR should always be at a higher level, three to four times higher than the prospect.

At this point we have several possibilities for the calculation of the MROR. It can be a return on capital, assets or equity or a DCFR. Because the DCFR and GRR relate to cash flow effects, they are preferable for screening prospects. They deal with the actual effects on the corporate treasury of making the investment. A cash flow analysis represents the real world of cash inflow and outflow.

The Two Components of Minimum Rate

In the real world, however, there are other influences. The principal influence is explained by the following equation.

$$\text{Minimum rate of return} = b + r$$

where:

    b = the return on an AAA bond
    r = the risk premium for the investment

This equation gives a general but abstract concept involving the minimum return. The factor b is the safe return that any investor can get while r reflects the *perceived* risk of the investor. Risky investments require higher returns, on the average, because they are perceived as being less safe than the always available investment in a high yield bond.

It is important to realize that both b and r are market determined. It is much easier to see this fact in the case of the corporate bond than it is in the case of the perceived risk. A corporate bond will only yield an interest rate that influences a buyer to purchase that bond. Its rate is definitely market determined. How, then, is the risk premium r market determined?

Consider an offshore sale in Federal waters. It is a sealed bidding and many companies compete. If a given company decided, unilaterally, to bid at a high rate of return it might not get any tracts in the sale. In other words, its perceived risk was so much higher than the market that it bought no tracts. Consider the opposite case. If the perceived risk of a company is considerably below that of competition, it will purchase more tracts than originally envisioned. And if the competition (market) is right, in its collective judgments, the company will lose money—its return was not set high enough.

There is also a hidden market in most companies. It is the board of directors. Its perceived risk often affects the minimum rate of return. If a specific division is doing well, with high rates of return, management may well ask "Can't you spend more money in this division?" In other words, the board's perceived risk is low for this division. On the other hand, a division with low rates of return will probably be reviewed to see if too much money is being spent in the area or its minimum rate of return will be raised because management's perceived risk is high for the division.

Overall, the MROR should be close to the value of expected earnings for the corporation in the near future. Otherwise, you dilute return on capital and risk lower future earnings per share. The explorer may well find a high-risk premium attached to his riskier investments. This attachment can occur even if the investment has been (in the eyes of the analyst) properly risked. If every investment was, indeed, properly risked the MROR would apply equally to all similar investments. However, as every explorer knows, the degree of uncertainty in geologic data enables many a manager to apply his own perceived risk adjustments.

You can see that an expectation of future returns on investment does relate to the cost of capital, and that the rate of reinvestment can raise or lower future returns on assets. Thus, even future earnings must be viewed in terms of what unusual factors might either raise or depress them abnormally.

One final factor must be considered. Prospect economics do not include all exploratory costs, even if properly risked. Examples would be allocated overhead, administrative costs, research costs or regional seismic lines unrelated to specific prospects. Therefore, the return desired from drilling prospects should compensate for the slightly lower expenditures used. Such an upward adjustment to the MROR would normally be modest.

Minimum Rate, Prime Rate and Inflation

The historic relationship between inflation, prime rate and an estimate of industry's MROR range is shown in Fig. 8–1. The period covered is 1960 to the mid-1980s. The prime rate has almost always been larger than the rate of inflation and the industry's MROR has been historically about 4 to 5 percentage points above the prime rate. In this figure we see the real world relationship between the MROR and the one measure we have of the cost of capital—the prime rate. The correlation is approximate, but the relative trends are there. The main point of Fig. 8–1 is that the MROR does bear a rough relationship to the prime rate and thus to inflation.

Deciding what should be the minimum rate of return is a decision that ought to be properly related to expected returns on equity, assets or capital, even if the means for expressing that minimum is the DCFR. In any case, it should be set so that a company can make investments in the good, often one-time opportunities that come its way, as well as provide for future growth.

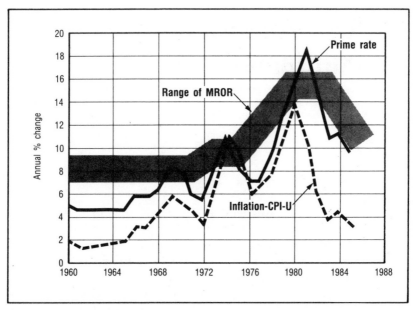

Fig. 8–1   General correlation between prime rate, MROR and inflation (courtesy AAPG *Explorer*)

REFERENCES

1. Megill, Robert E., "Minimum Rate of Return Varies with Economy,"
   AAPG *Explorer*, Jan. 1986.
2. Megill, Robert E., "Prime Rate May Indicate MROR," AAPG *Explorer*,
   Feb. 1986.
3. Megill, Robert E., "MROR A Long-Term Proposition," AAPG *Explorer*,
   March 1986.

9 Risk Analysis— Fundamentals

You might think at this point that you are ready to embark on the evaluation of exploration investments; but we haven't discussed one of the most important items in our evaluations—risk. It is the purpose of the next two chapters to take economics out of cost, where we've been for almost eight chapters, into risk.

The most important single variable in the evaluation of exploratory investments is risk. It is the one factor about which others can tell you the least. In the search for hydrocarbons, facts are few and decisions must always be made before all facts are known. Because of the many unknown factors, we depend a lot on experience in exploration. But the wise explorer knows that the facts, though few, are always worth reviewing.

Only two chapters in this book are devoted to risk analysis. In reality the subject of risk analysis deserves much more space. However, any introductory text must limit discussions to basic fundamentals. For those interested in an expansion of Chapters 9 and 10, a companion volume is available. It is entitled *An Introduction to Risk Analysis*, 2nd edition published in 1984.[1]

Risk vs. Uncertainty

Many people equate risk to uncertainty. In this chapter we will make a distinction between the two. We shall always use risk to mean an opportunity for loss. The term uncertainty shall apply to factors where the outcome is not certain but where the opportunity for loss is not as apparent as in risk.

The chances for loss are easy to distinguish in an exploratory well. Statistics alone show loss to be more normal than gain. In an investment evaluation, however, there are numerous uncertainties

140

regarding such things as legislation, interfuel competition, etc. These factors affect the economics but few have the outright opportunity for loss possible in exploratory risk.

Quantifying Risk in Exploration

If you put down a rough formula to describe the economics of exploration, it might look as follows:

Hydrocarbon potential + Economics + Risk = Decision

You may wish to substitute prospect or play for the first item; but regardless of the first term, we take geological-geophysical concepts involving hydrocarbons, determine the economic consequences of these concepts and apply risk. To this point we have assumed hydrocarbon potential, shown methods for calculating economics, and we now approach the subject of risk.

We shall show ways to quantify the risks of exploration. In so doing, we always face the possibility of quantifying ignorance, or bias, or both. However, decisions are made every day in exploration based on mental quantification. Such quantification relates to one man's experience. His "long shot" may be another's "fair chance" or another man's "risky." We need some standard method to gain comparable definitions of risk for the same prospect. Quantification at least offers the hope of more consistency in expressing risk. It should also encourage the quantifier to review his basis for establishing risk and in so doing reduce errors of oversight.

Looking at Fig. 9–1, we see a simple probability scale. The abscissa shows numbers from zero to 1.0. The 1.0 point on the right side of the figure indicates a probability of 100% or certainty. On the other hand, on the left side of Fig. 9–1, the zero point means the event won't happen—a probability of occurrence of zero. Using this simple

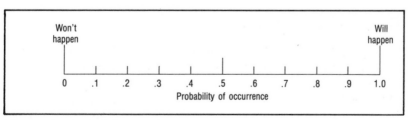

Fig. 9–1 Probability scale

scale to indicate the chance of occurrence is much more definitive. Even though used subjectively, the value of the probability scale is that it conveys uniform meaning. We all understand what a 50-50 chance means. A 70% chance conveys much more meaning than "..close to a sure thing!" Finally, the use of probability allows us to perform other important calculations that we cannot with mere words such as "good", "poor", "excellent", etc.

Risk Defined by Probabilities

Before delving into exploratory risks, two fundamental laws of probability will be briefly reviewed.

Probability theory considers all possible happenings and attempts then to estimate the most likely happening. Even though the theory usually has meaning only if there are a significant number of happenings, it can teach us important things about few happenings. It can help us estimate the odds.

As we have found in other chapters on other subjects, some new terms are required. In probability theory, we need to know the following:

An *event*—is one of two or more things which may occur in a given situation.
An *outcome*—is the thing which does occur. One thinks in terms of events before the fact and outcomes after the fact.
Probability—is a statement of the frequency of a specific event being the outcome after repeated trials. It is expressed as a per cent or a fraction.

The fundamental rules of probability are:

The addition rule and the multiplication rule. Both rules will be illustrated by rolling dice.

The Addition Rule

What is the probability of rolling a five on one roll of one die?
There are six possible events: 1, 2, 3, 4, 5, and 6. So the probability of rolling a five is one in six or one-sixth ($\frac{1}{6}$). Expressed as a percentage there is a 16.7% chance of rolling a five in one roll of one die. Note that when any one of the six possible events does occur it excludes the other five possibilities. These events are thus mutually

exclusive. The addition rule says that the probability that one or another of two or more mutually exclusive events will occur is the sum of their separate probabilities.

We can review the rule by considering more than one event. What is the probability of rolling a two or a five on one roll of one die? Reading P(5) as the "probability of five" our question is:

$$P(2 \text{ or } 5) = ?$$

The two events are mutually exclusive, so we can apply the addition rule.

$$P(2) = \frac{1}{6}$$
$$P(5) = \frac{1}{6}$$
$$P(2 \text{ or } 5) = P(2) + P(5)$$
$$= \frac{1}{6} + \frac{1}{6}$$
$$= \frac{1}{3}$$
$$= 33.3\%$$

The Multiplication Rule

When two dice are rolled, the outcome of either die is not affected by the other. The outcomes are independent of each other. The multiplication rule states that: the probability of two independent events having specific outcomes is the product of their separate probabilities.

Consider the question, "What is the probability of rolling a double five on one roll of two dice?"

$$P(5,5) = ?$$

The event of a five showing on one die is independent of a five on the other die. Thus the multiplication rule applies.

$$P(5) = \frac{1}{6}$$
$$P(5,5) = P(5) \times P(5)$$
$$= \frac{1}{6} \times \frac{1}{6}$$
$$= \frac{1}{36}$$
$$= 2.8\%$$

Probabilities and the Search for Hydrocarbons

The search for hydrocarbons is by its very nature a function of complex probabilities. One can summarize these probabilities in a threefold generalization.

Geologists and geophysicists are concerned first of all with the probability that hydrocarbons do exist in a specific geographic area. Second, they are concerned with the probability of being able to find these hydrocarbon deposits. Third, they must be concerned with the probability of whether the deposits found will be economic.[2]

Are Hydrocarbons Present?

In every unexplored basin, geologists have been faced with the basic question, "Are hydrocarbons present?" The only final answer to this question is the wildcat well; but in order to justify an exploratory well, the geologist looks for reasons why hydrocarbons could be present. He may try comparing the unexplored basin to a similar but explored basin. He will look for optimum sedimentary depositional environments, lithologic seals, trap forming mechanisms, etc.

We will deal very lightly with economic approaches to this basic question (see Chapter 12). The assessment of an unexplored basin must begin as a geologic interpretation and economic calculations can be handled simply until more data are available.

Will You Find Them?

After oil or gas is discovered, the question becomes, "If hydrocarbons are present, will you find them?" The answer to this question involves much more than technical skill. Land ownership, degree of competition, available capital, timing of lease sales and many other factors affect what a given concern can accomplish. Technical skill without the backing of land and money to explore that land is of no value.

If Found, Are They Economic?

The probabilities here involve size, amount of revenue generation possible (deliverability) and costs. Chapter 12 will deal extensively with combinations of these factors. Later in this chapter we will comment on field size. For now we shall return to what we can call "wildcat" risk. Chapter 10 deals with economic risk.

Wildcat Risk

If we modify our general formula to: Prospect + Economics + Risk = Decision, several significant illustrations involving risk and probability are possible. We chose the prospect because most of the explorationists' efforts relate to specific prospects. Our definition of wildcat risk, then, is the chance a prospect has of making a discovery.

For illustration purposes we shall use a very simplified method for quantifying wildcat risk. A few very complex procedures have been suggested. A recommendation by Schwade[3] includes five pages of a prospect check list. His suggestions pertain to the geologic factors which make up wildcat risk. No one knows exactly what conditions produce the most favorable chance of all geologic factors acting favorably; because of this fact, we will never have a uniform agreement on what constitutes wildcat risk.

There are numerous obvious factors affecting the trapping of hydrocarbons and one's ability to map them. Some important examples are subsurface control, type of trap, quality of basic data, nearness to production or shows, and many others. An ideal system would isolate all pertinent factors, assign probabilities to them and combine them into a composite risk factor. Our simplified method can be made more complex. It is used herein for illustration purposes only. Anyone interested in additional research on prospect risking will find ample reference in the literature.[1,4,5]

Simplified Method for Estimating Composite Geologic Risk

Our method will concern itself with three factors only, which shall be assumed to encompass all geologic conditions favorable for hydrocarbon entrapment. These factors are:

1. *Structure.* This factor shall encompass faulting, type of trap, seal, geophysical control and quality, subsurface control, etc.
2. *Reservoir.* This factor shall include rock properties, depositional conditions, and other factors specifically affecting a productive reservoir.
3. *Environment.* This factor shall include paleohistory, timing aspects, proximity of source beds, shows, etc.

One final thought on factors affecting wildcat risk. Data will vary from prospect to prospect and an absolutely uniform system cannot always be used. In the absence of adequate data you may settle for estimating only the first two—structure and reservoirs. If you cannot reasonably assess a factor, leave it out. Note the modifying term "reasonably." You are always dealing in uncertainties in estimating probabilities; but you must assess some factors (say structure and reservoirs) otherwise you have no prospect.

We are now ready to illustrate the developing of a number which will represent a geologist's best estimate of a prospect's chances of being a discovery. We shall consider our three factors more or less independent of each other. Remembering the multiplication rule, our steps to estimate wildcat risk become:

1. Isolate critical geologic factors (which we have defined here as three).
2. Estimate each factor's chance of being favorable.
3. Multiply the per cent chances of all factors together.

The product is an estimate of the overall chance of success; it is an estimate of the probability of all geologic factors occurring favorably simultaneously.

What Can You Learn from Past Wildcats?

If you have never considered this approach, you may wish to conduct some useful research first. Check the last 10 to 20 rank wildcats drilled. Fifty would be a better sample, but you may not have drilled that many. We shall assume you have made such an analysis and use the results to demonstrate our method of risking. Suppose your research of 50 wildcats results in the following data:

Wells Finding	No. of Wells
Structure as predicted	35
Good reservoir conditions	25
Optimum environment	41

These figures tell us that:

1. Structural predictions were correct 70% of the time.
2. Only 50% of the time were good reservoirs present.
3. About 80% of the time the proper environment was present.

Your historic wildcat risk should be about (remember the multiplication rule):

$$0.7 \times 0.5 \times 0.8 = 0.28 = 28\%$$

If this factor is near your success rate (if you have 14 discoveries) your data reasonably measured the critical geologic factors.

Your research makes two important contributions. If data were sufficient you now have a glimpse of history and its relevant probabilities. If your data were insufficient, you need to begin recording estimates and critical factors. It is by carefully reviewing what was estimated under uncertainty that you can hope to sharpen your predictions.

Method Applied to a Single Prospect

One can apply the technique to a single prospect to estimate its probability of having favorable geologic conditions. We shall again use the School prospect shown in Fig. 9–2 contoured on top of the objective formation.

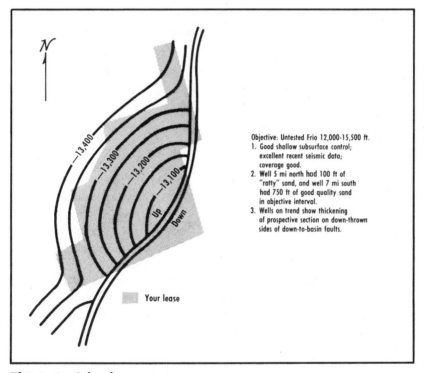

Objective: Untested Frio 12,000-15,500 ft.
1. Good shallow subsurface control; excellent recent seismic data; coverage good.
2. Well 5 mi north had 100 ft of "ratty" sand, and well 7 mi south had 750 ft of good quality sand in objective interval.
3. Wells on trend show thickening of prospective section on down-thrown sides of down-to-basin faults.

Your lease

Fig. 9–2   School prospect

Note the factual information on the right side of the figure. Using these facts about the School prospect, an explorationist's thinking might be as follows:

"Hum...the structure is tied down well so it should have a 75-80% chance of being as predicted. Now the reservoir conditions look like a fair shot; however, at this depth our experience in finding good sand has been poor—maybe a 40-50% chance? The Frio is a known producing formation in the area, although this particular fault segment has turned up nothing large so far. Timing and migration, no problems here—say 85% chance."

The foregoing thoughts could be translated and recorded on an appraisal form as follows:

Wildcat Appraisal

Prospect:	School	Proposed T D:	15,500 feet
Location:	Nonesuch	Objective:	Frio
		Interval:	12,000 feet-TD

Risk Estimation

1. Structure	50, 60, 70, 80, 90	77	Composite
2. Reservoirs	30, 40, 50, 60, 70	45	risk
3. Environment	60, 70, 80, 90, 100	85	factor

0.29*

*0.77 × 0.45 × 0.85 = 0.29

The composite risk factor—the chance of success—is now a synthesis of the geologist's judgments about critical factors. He has had to review his data and record his opinions. Note that the form has numbers in the middle column with one number underlined. The underlined numbers are those from your research and are placed on the form for relevance but not as absolute guidelines. One's ability to predict critical factors may change, you may be estimating in a different trend, in a relatively unexplored area, etc. However, if your estimates consistently depart from prior historic results, you need to examine the cause. You are either establishing new history or your estimating may not be in the ballpark.

The composite risk factor is expressed as a single figure—0.29. There is probably no risk difference between 0.27 or 0.29; furthermore it is difficult to say how much difference is required to be meaningful.

When you have numerous prospects to appraise, however, a method of establishing a composite risk is useful and necessary for risk ranking. The estimate is subjective and we shall find uses for its quantification in our calculations involving economic risk to be shown in Chapter 10.

Before leaving the illustration on wildcat appraisal, note the estimated chances of occurrence of key geologic controls. For structure the number was 77 indicating a 77% chance of adequacy for the structural mapping. Actually, the best usage of this form would be to limit the probabilities to just one digit. The second digit implies an accuracy that does not exist. Thus, the structural chance should be rounded to 0.8, the reservoir adequacy to 0.4 and the environment to 0.9. The prospect chance of having hydrocarbons present then becomes $0.8 \times 0.4 \times 0.9 = 0.288$ or .29 or 29%. The answer is the same, but the accuracy implied is more realistic.

Before proceeding to economic risk, two additional facets must be examined. They are statistical success and field size distributions. Both terms relate to techniques which have applications in making decisions on exploration investments.

Statistical Success

Explorationists usually ponder how often success will be achieved from a given program of wildcats. A company drilling 20 or 30 wildcats per year might want to know the chances of making one, two, three or five discoveries. Keep in mind that the word "discovery" used here means simply a producing well. How much is discovered will be discussed under field size distributions.

To find the chance of success, a mathematical technique called *binomial* (two numbers) *expansion* is used. To simplify matters we shall assume each well in the program has the same chance of success. As explorationists we know that some prospects have better odds than others; but for most exploration programs, we can assume an average success rate with reasonable safety.

Our symbols will be:

$$D = \text{Probability of a dry hole}$$
$$S = \text{Probability of success}$$

For one well

$$D + S = 1.0 \qquad\qquad \text{(Eq. 9–1)}$$

We can also write

$$D + S = (D + S)^1$$

For a two-well program, see Fig. 9–3; there are four possible outcomes and our equation becomes:

$$DD + DS + SD + SS = 1.0 \qquad\qquad \text{(Eq. 9–2)}$$

Of course DS + SD can be written as 2 DS which allows us to write the probabilities for two wells as follows:

$$D^2 + 2DS + S^2 = 1.0 \qquad\qquad \text{(Eq. 9–3)}$$

If you remember your algebra, $D^2 + 2\,DS + S^2$ is the product of $(D + S) \times (D + S)$ and can be written as $(D + S)^2$. Therefore,

$$D^2 + 2DS + S^2 = (D + S)^2 \qquad\qquad \text{(Eq. 9–4)}$$

The left half of Eq. 9–4 is the expansion of the binomial $(D + S)$ to $(D + S)^2$.

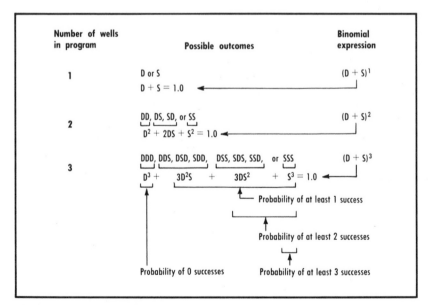

Fig. 9–3   Binomial expansion

The mathematics associated with binomial expansion is easy only if the numbers are small or simple. For example if you assume D and S have an equal chance (50% probability) and you drill only two wells, then DD + DS + SD + SS tells us that:

You have a 25% chance of drilling two dry holes (DD).
You have a 50% chance of drilling only one successful well (DS + SD).
You have a 25% chance of drilling two discoveries (SS), and
You have a 75% chance of at least one discovery (DS + SD + SS).

However, when you go to larger numbers of wells and other probabilities for D & S (success rates), the math becomes much more complex. Consider the binomial expansion for a five-well program which is:

$$D^5 + 5 D^4 S + 10 D^3 S^2 + 10 D^2 S^3 + 5 DS^4 + S^5 = 1.0$$

Fortunately for all of us most textbooks on statistics or manuals of statistical series have tables on binomial probabilities related to the number of trials (number of wells in a program). The tables show individual probabilities (the chance of exactly x successes in an N well program) or cumulative terms (the chance of x or more success in an N well program). From these tables graphs can be constructed to show the probabilities for various numbers of discoveries, given certain wildcat success rates. Fig. 9–4 is such a graph. It assumes a 10% success rate. If we have a 20-well program, the graph tells us that our chance of:

At least one (one or more) discovery	is 88%	88 in 100
At least two discoveries	is 61%	3 in 5
At least three discoveries	is 32%	1 in 3
At least four discoveries	is 13%	1 in 8

The chance of drilling any number of dry holes in succession can be determined from the "≥ 1 discovery" curve ($\geq$ means equal to or greater than; or you can think of it as the curve showing the chances of *at least* x discoveries—in the case referred to here—the chance of at least *one* discovery). The chance of one dry hole "in succession" is (1.00 − 0.10) or 0.90 or 90%. For additional wells read the value on the $\geq$ 1 curve and subtract from 1.00; examples are:

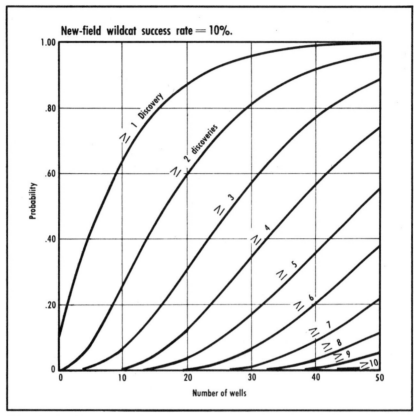

Fig. 9—4 Cumulative binomial probability

2 dry holes in succession	=	81%	4 in 5
5 dry holes in succession	=	59%	3 in 5
10 dry holes in succession	=	35%	1 in 3
20 dry holes in succession	=	12%	1 in 8

One can state the last point another way. At a 10% success rate, even in drilling 20 holes we still face a 12% chance that all are dry.

These illustrations should give you some idea of the limitations of a single success percentage, even from only a mathematical viewpoint. The binomial expansion also provides additional information about risks at given success rates. It is from a binomial expansion that we get concepts about required exposure for a reasonable probability of success and insights into "Gambler's Ruin" concepts.[1]

The Normal Distribution

Now some comments on distributions. A distribution is an orderly arrangement of similar things.

The arrangement relates to a common characteristic of interest. Fig. 9–5 is frequency distribution of the heights of a sample of women. In this plot the group of similar things is women and the common characteristic is height. The bar graph of Fig. 9–5 is sometimes called a *histogram* (history + graph). Histograms plot class intervals versus their relative frequencies. In Fig. 9–5 the class interval is the height group and each bar shows the number of women whose heights range from 61½ to 62½ (in this sample of 1,345 women) is 186.

If we feel this sample is typical of all other women, the chart can be used to predict heights of women not measured in the sample. We must believe, however, that the sample is typical.

The shape of the distribution in Fig. 9–5 is similar to many others. In fact this shape is found so frequently that it is called the normal distribution—also the "bell shaped" curve when drawn as a continuous function. It has most of its values grouped in the middle range with fewer and fewer toward two extremes.

If percentages rather than absolute values are used on the Y axis, a probability distribution results; such a distribution is indicated by the

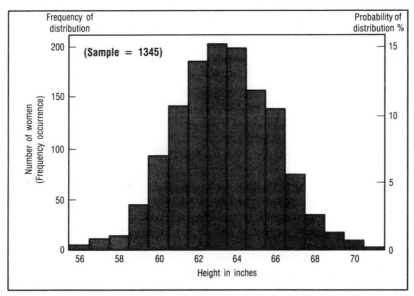

Fig. 9–5   Heights of women

scale to the right in Fig. 9–5. This scale shows the Y axis representing the probability of occurrence. In the sample 13.8% of the women (186 ÷ 1,345 × 100) are between 61½ and 62½ inches. Assuming that our sample is typical, every time a woman is measured for height, there is a 13.8% chance it will fall between 61½ and 62½ inches.

Adding the values of Fig. 9–5 cumulatively produces a cumulative probability distribution shown in Fig. 9–6. The Y axis now shows the probability of a woman from this sample being taller or shorter than a certain height.

Straight lines are easier to work with than curved lines and a particular kind of graph paper is available for probability plots. A probability grid is shown in Fig. 9–7. The Y axis has been changed in such a way that cumulative probability values of normal distributions fall in a straight line.

All these comments have been leading toward a particular distribution useful to explorationists.

Nature's Group of Fields

One of the basic reference points in a mature trend is the size of existing fields.

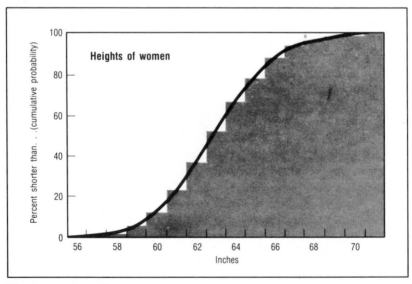

Fig. 9–6 Cumulative probability distribution

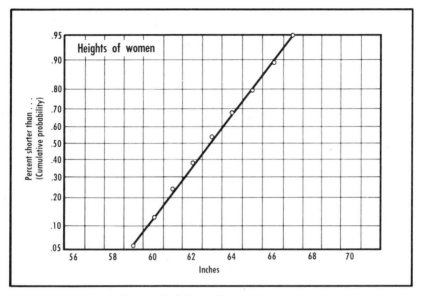

Fig. 9–7 Cumulative probability distribution

It is well documented that, within a given geologic unit (basin or formation) field size exhibits a specific frequency distribution.[6] If you plot frequency of occurrence versus the logarithm of field size, the resultant histogram is similar in shape to a normal distribution. Since the logarithm of the variable is plotted, the distribution is called a *lognormal distribution.* This natural arrangement can be used to describe and understand the distribution of oil and gas accumulations within the earth's crust.

Constructing a Field Size Distribution (FSD) Plot

First, however, let's demonstrate, in a very simple way, how one constructs a FSD plot. The steps are as follows:

1. Arrange all fields, ranking them by size, with the largest field first, the smallest field last.
2. To the total number of fields, add one. If n is the total number of listed fields, this instruction means (n + 1). The (n + 1) number is the denominator of the fraction to be used to calculate cumulative percentages.
3. To calculate the cumulative frequency percentages (for plotting purposes) take the first ranked field (the largest) and plot

it on logprobability paper at the percentage described by the fraction (fractile) 1/(n + 1).

4. The second field ranked is plotted at 2/(n + 1); the third is plotted at 3/(n + 1), etc—with the smallest field plotted at n/(n + 1).

5. Connect the fields by a straight line (a best fit line) to illustrate cumulative frequency.

We can demonstrate these steps with just a few fields. Given five fields of sizes 38, 160, 72, 10 and 20, we construct Table 9–1 as outlined in the four steps above.

TABLE 9–1

Calculating Plot Points For a Field Size Distribution

No. Fields	Arrange By Size	Fractile %
1	160	16
2	72	33
3	38	50
4	20	67
5	10	83

The appropriate data from Table 9–1, columns two and three, are plotted in Fig. 9–8. The graph utilizes lognormal probability paper. A straight line on such paper indicates a lognormal distribution. The graphs are frequently shown rotated 90°. The rotation reverses the slope, but yields the same information about the distribution.

Some Facts about Lognormal Graph Paper

Other than the fact it shows a straight line, why use lognormal paper?

First, we know that nature most normally groups fields by this distribution if the sample is large enough. Thus, we should plot field size data on lognormal paper to see if the sample is adequate.

Second, since we have a firm idea of the configuration of distribution, we can use this relationship to our advantage for implied or inferred distributions. When we begin to estimate prospect size in Chapter 10, some inferred distributions will be utilized.

Now, what can we observe about this distribution assuming that it truly reflects a larger sample and the entire population?

1. The median size is 38 BCF. One-half of the discoveries are larger than this size and one-half are smaller.
2. The construction of the graph paper is such that it clusters discoveries around the median. This clustering serves to demonstrate the size concentration. Note that 60% of the fields (between 20 and 80% lines) will have sizes between 12 and 130 billion cu. ft.
3. The effect of the log plot can be demonstrated by these same numbers. The 30% of the fields from 80% to 50% show a field size increase from 12 to 38 or an increase of 26 billion cu. ft. In contrast the same number of fields from 50% to 20% probability shows an increase from 38 to 130 billion cu. ft. or an increase of 92, almost 3.5 times the volume change on the low side of the median.
4. The log plot means that there are fewer big discoveries than small ones.
5. The weighted average (mean) is 60 billion cu. ft., 22 billion cu. ft. larger than the median. The mean will always exceed the median in a lognormal distribution because the upper half of plotted points is proportionately larger, i.e., the X axis is logarithmic.

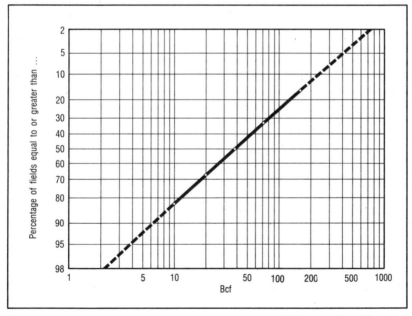

Fig. 9–8   Cumulative frequency distribution (field size distribution)

Using FSD Plots for Calculating Chances of Finding a Specific Field Size

Field size varies more or less continually from zero to the largest in the basin.

Because of this fact, the chance of finding a field of a specific size is near zero. In spite of this fact, one can use FSD charts to determine the approximate chance of finding fields near specific values.

Remember of course that a FSD graph deals with discoveries only. Data from the graph must be multiplied times the success ratio to determine the chance of success.

Using the curve of Fig. 9–8, what is the chance of finding a 50 billion cu. ft. or larger discovery in a play where the "going" success rate is 20%? From Fig. 9–8 we see that 43% of the fields are equal to or greater than 50 billion cu. ft. Then what are our probable chances—if we get a discovery? Since there's only a 20% chance you will be successful the chance of finding a 50 billion cu. ft. field or larger is:

$$.43 \times .20 = .086$$

Based on our FSD graph, only 8.6% of the time will a well find at least 50 billion cu. ft., or 2 chances in 25.

The chances of finding at least a 10 billion cu. ft. discovery (at 20% success) are:

$$.83 \times .20 = 0.166$$

You have one chance in six of getting a discovery equal to or greater than 10 billion cu. ft. at a 20% success rate.

You may have only a small exploration program in an area or a trend. Furthermore, you may have your prospects already selected with no more acreage available. In such cases you are dealing with specific data, not samples of a large population. Field size distributions may, under these special circumstances, seem of little value. Nevertheless, FSDs are very useful in maintaining a touch with reality when estimating size; and if you plan exploration programs in mature trends, your view of your potential discoveries will be more meaningful if you understand nature's distribution of oil and gas fields in that play.

REVIEW

This chapter covers a few basic concepts associated with wildcat risk. Probability theory helps us combine geologic fact and opinion in ways which clarify our best estimate of risk. Where we have sufficient data, statistical analysis and field size distributions help us understand the odds.

We are now ready to combine risking techniques with economics to determine profitability. The combination gives us risk-weighted profitability.

BIBLIOGRAPHY

1. Megill, R.E., *An Introduction to Risk Analysis,* 2nd Edition, PennWell Publishing Co., Tulsa, Okla., 1984.
2. Megill, R.E., "How to Measure Exploration Profits," *Oil & Gas Journal,* March 18, 1968, p. 126.
3. Schwade, Irving T., 1967, "Geologic Quantification: Description-Numbers-Success Ratio," AAPG Bulletin, Vol. 51, p. 1225-1239.
4. Rummerfield, Ben J. and Morrisey, Norman S., "How to Evaluate Exploration Prospects," *World Oil,* April 1965, p. 126.
5. Campbell, W.M., "Risk Analysis Overall Chance of Success Related to Number of Ventures," paper given at 36th Annual Fall Meeting of SPE of AIME, October 1961.
6. Kaufman, Gordon M., "Statistical Decision and Related Techniques in Oil and Gas Exploration," 1962 Ford Foundation Doctorial Dissertation Series.

PROBLEMS

1. From field sizes shown below, construct a field-size distribution plot on lognormal probability paper.
2. What is the average field size?
3. Given a 20% success rate, what are the chances of finding at least a 50 million barrel oil field (or larger)?

Field Sizes for Nine Fields
Millions of Barrels

3.5
160
35
22
13.5
90
7.5
350
55

10 Risk Analysis—Applications

Numbers are useful abstractions. They allow us to investigate ideas and concepts otherwise impossible, but they also offer the illusion of precision. Perhaps the previous chapter will serve to illustrate that such words as success rate and field size, although often represented by a single number, more accurately describe a range of numbers.

We shall be looking at specific numbers and ranges of possible numbers. The risks of wildcat success will be combined with additional uncertainties into economic risk. Even with compounding uncertainties in these estimates, the goal is to learn more about the investments we make. In the absence of complete knowledge, we describe only what we know; but that is an important start.

Economic Risk

In this chapter we shall incorporate the knowledge from all previous chapters to arrive at risk-weighted profitability—the end point for any exploratory evaluation. Risk weighting is important to the explorationist because the most probable outcome from his efforts is a dry hole. The definition of a dry hole eludes accurate description. The offshore areas of the U.S. have numerous wells classified as economically dry. They contained oil or gas (often enough to be termed a discovery on land) but in insufficient quantities to pay for platforms and related expenses. A dry hole, then, can be absolutely dry—no oil or gas—or can intimate teasing amounts of noncommercial hydrocarbons.

Begin with Hydrocarbon Estimates

The introduction of field size distributions in Chapter 9 demonstrated the wide range of possible field sizes in a productive geologic trend.

Yet one of the first things we need to know is "What size field?" In previous chapters we have shown a finite cash flow stream for the successful School prospect; but until the outcome (successful or dry) we need to recognize that other possible sizes for the School prospect could have given us other cash flow streams—some larger, some smaller.

The "Most Likely" Size

Whenever we settle on a single field size, it can be thought of as our "most likely" case.

By some method we have singled out specific values for the critical parameters of size and multiplied these to get our "best guess" estimate. The most likely case can be the product of:

Net pay × recovery per ft. of pay × productive area

Our singled-out values would then be a specific pay thickness, recovery factor and areal extent. Suppose for a Typical prospect in a play we assume 1,000 productive acres with 100 feet of sand having a recovery of 1.0 $\overline{\text{Mcf}}$/acre-ft. Then:

1,000 acres × 100 feet × 1.0 $\overline{\text{Mcf}}$/acre-ft. = 100 billion cu. ft.

In Chapter 5 the methods were shown to convert such a reserve into dollars. The School prospect served as the reference field. To refresh your memory, the steps to determine this value were:

1. Calculation of the investment outflow. We listed the exploration and development investments by year and developed their after-tax cash flow.
2. From a production schedule, an inflow of revenue, after tax, was generated.
3. The investment and revenue cash flows were combined for the net cash flow, after tax.
4. Discount factors were applied, in Chapter 6, Table 6–5, to the annual cash flows to get the DCFR and present value at various discount rates.

Only one of many possible cash flows for the School prospect was calculated. The absolute probability of obtaining our most likely case is near zero. We made judgments for each critical variable to produce our most likely case, but having only one case limits what we should know about an investment. What other possibilities are there? How probable is their outcome?

Payoff Table

The payoff table answers some of these questions and it represents a good starting point to consider other possible cases. It is from the payoff table that we get expected value.

In considering expected value, we follow a series of steps, each of which requires either a judgment or some information relating to a judgment. These steps are:

1. List the possible outcomes.
2. By each outcome, list its probability of occurrence.
3. Show the economic consequence of this occurrence.
4. Multiply the consequences times the probability of occurrence.
5. Sum the products.

We can illustrate this concept by means of the Typical prospect previously assigned a reserve size of 100 billion cu. ft. For convenience sake we will assign it the composite risk factor of the School prospect which was 0.29 (Chapter 9); the two outcomes, then, are:

Dry hole	0.71
100 billion cu. ft.	0.29

We must calculate two economic assumptions to go with the two outcomes. First, let's assume an AFIT cost of a dry hole as $1.5 million. Second, we will assume that our calculation of PVP at 10% for the 100 billion cu. ft. was $7.5 million. Following the steps outlined above we have:

TABLE 10-1

Payoff Table
Typical Prospect

Outcome	Probability	PVP @ 10%, $M	Risk weighted PVP @ 10%, $M
Dry hole	0.71	−1,500	−1.065
100 billion cu. ft.	0.29	7,500	2,175
Total	1.00		1,110

This arrangement of expected value combines risk and present value and is often referred to as a "payoff" table. The discovery well may or may not be in the zero year. In the case of the School prospect it was not in year zero. For convenience sake, in the illustration of the Typical prospect the zero year is assumed. The AFIT dry hole cost is thus an undiscounted number.

The expected value of the two possible events (shown under the column headed *outcome*) is $1.11 million if we consider only the well cost as the total investment for the dry case. It is the expected payoff for the situation stated— assuming it could be repeated many times. Remember, a probability has been assigned to the PVP at 10%; we have calculated the PVP of a given reserve size, then estimated its probability of happening. Our expected value reflects our estimate of risk for a specific size field and a dry hole. If our estimates are correct and we can drill many Typical prospects, we should average a gain of $1.11 million per prospect (plus 10% since our $7.5 million is a PVP at 10%). Finally, there is no implication that this particular value is frequent, probable or even possible. It represents an average risk-weighted value. It has been adjusted by our judgments about the probability of possible outcomes.

Multiple Cases

Field size distributions help us realize that using just one possible size restricts our view of a prospect's economic potential.

We need a range of cases to depict more accurately the Typical prospect. To keep the illustration simple, a minimum and maximum case will be used. The probability of these additional occurrences must be determined and related with our most likely case to a successful outcome. The sum of their probabilities must add to 0.29. Cash flows for the other cases must be constructed and discounted. The results might be as shown in Table 10-2.

TABLE 10-2

Payoff Table
Typical Prospect

Outcome	Reserve-Bcf	Probability	PVP @ 10%, $M	Risk Weighted PVP @ 10%, $M
Dry hole	0	0.71	−1,500	−1,065
Minimum	30	0.09	−100	−9
Most likely	100	0.18	7,500	1,350
Maximum	400	0.02	30,500	610
Total		1.00		886

The addition of the minimum-maximum cases tripled our evaluation work but gave new information.

1. The expected value is now only $886,000. The decrease of $224,000 results from considering two additional reserve sizes, one smaller, one larger than the most likely size.
2. The expected value is very sensitive to the probability assigned the largest reserve. A 0.04 probability for the 400 billion cu. ft. case yields a risk-weighted PVP at 10% of $1.22 million. This small change in probability (if the probability of the most likely size remains unchanged and the probability for the minimum case is reduced to 0.07) will by itself increase the expected value to $1,498,000.
3. The minimum reserve, 30 billion cu. ft., has a present value loss at 10%. From this fact we can estimate the minimum profitable reserve size—it must be slightly larger than 30 billion cu. ft. Keep in mind that this limit is based on our value of money at 10%. If we valued money at 20%, a much larger reserve size would be required. If we valued money at only 8%, then 25 billion cu. ft. might be an acceptable size.
4. Table 10–2 also allows the calculations of a risk-weighted reserve as shown in Table 10–3.

TABLE 10–3

Risk-Weighted Reserves

Outcome	Reserve bcf	Probability	Risk-weighted Reserve bcf	Alternate Probability	Risk-weighted Reserve bcf
Dry	0	0.71	0	0.71	0
Minimum	30	0.09	3	0.06	2
Most likely	100	0.18	18	0.18	18
Maximum	400	0.02	8	0.05	20
Total		1.00	29	1.00	40

The risk-weighted reserve for the Typical prospect is 29 billion cu. ft., even though we still consider the most likely reserve to be 100 billion cu. ft. Do not think of a risk-weighted reserve as in place reserves! Remember that number is a mixture of reserve size possibilities and estimates of the probability of their outcome.

An alternate probability for the minimum and maximum reserve is shown to illustrate the sensitivity to the probability assigned to the larger reserve. The increase to 0.05 for the larger reserve size changes the risk-weighted reserve to 40 BCF! The most likely size is still 100 billion cu. ft., however.

Note that our first set of probabilities yielded the same risk-weighted reserve as the most likely case when viewed as the only answer (100 billion cu. ft. × 0.29 = 29 billion cu. ft.).

Why risk-weight anything? There is no guarantee that the Typical prospect contains 29 billion cu. ft.; but we expect 100 Typical prospects to yield an average of 29 billion cu. ft. and $1.11 million (PVP at 10%) per prospect.

The value of risk-weighting anything, including field sizes, is to define an unknown quantity with greater accuracy—or to show the limits of one's feelings or judgments about various sizes, probabilities or conditions. There is also the underlying assumption that you have numerous similar opportunities.

A payoff table can also be used to compare the expected value for various choices.[1] Typical examples are the expected value for:

1. Drilling a 100% working interest well versus a farmout of the tract retaining an override.
2. Drilling a 100% well versus some smaller working interest— or a small working interest plus an override.

The procedure is the same. The events and outcomes do not change; only the PVP changes under the various ownerships assumed.

Multiple Variables

Perhaps you feel more at home estimating the probability of parameters which make up field size rather than field size itself.

Your familiarity here may produce better input data into your risking "model." Usually such a procedure introduces more cases and the need for a computer. We can show how cases quickly multiply when variables are introduced into field size parameters.

We could test a very simple expansion of our problem by assigning two variables to the three parameters which produce reserve size. These parameters are net feet of pay, recovery per acre-foot and productive area. Two values for three parameters produce eight cases—$2 \times 2 \times 2$ or 2^3. Most explorationists define their parameters at least by maximum, most likely and minimum values. Our choice, then, is three values for three parameters making 27 cases or reserve sizes—$3 \times 3 \times 3$ or 3^3. This expansion for the Typical prospect is as follows:

TABLE 10-4

Typical Prospect

Parameter	Value	Probability
Net pay-ft.	50	0.3
	100	0.5
	190	0.2
Recovery Per Acre-Ft.-$\overline{M}$cf	0.7	0.3
	1.0	0.6
	1.5	0.1
Productive area	800	0.3
	1,000	0.5
	1,400	0.2

The development of the 27 cases is illustrated by the probability tree diagram in Fig. 10-1. This diagram is the most elaborate and perhaps complex figure in the book. It contains, however, many useful relationships and concepts; and it is worth spending the time to uncover its meaning.

1. First of all it concerns only reserve sizes. However, it includes all possible sizes based on our assumptions.
2. The diagram begins with the decision to drill and shows all possible outcomes. Note the now familiar probabilities of 0.71 dry and 0.29 successful.
3. The first branches show a 71% chance of a dry hole and a 29% chance of a successful well—a gas discovery.
4. Branches from the gas discovery show a 30% chance of 50 ft. of pay, a 50% chance of 100 ft. and a 20% chance of 190 ft.
5. From each pay thickness are probabilities for recovery factors of 30% for 0.7 $\overline{M}$cf per acre-ft., 60% for 1.0 $\overline{M}$cf and 10% for 1.5 $\overline{M}$cf per acre-ft.
6. The final branching from recovery factors shows a 30% probability for a field size of 800 acres, 50% for 1,000 acres and a 20% probability of a field covering 1,400 acres.
7. Fig. 10-1 develops from the three variables for three parameters 27 reserve sizes ranging from 28 billion cu. ft. to 399 billion cu. ft.; and it shows the probability of occurrence of each size.
8. The sum of the 27 probabilities is 0.29—29% the chance of a discovery.

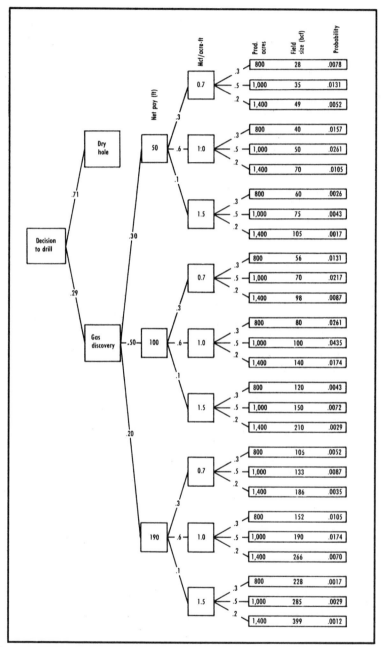

Fig. 10–1 Probability tree diagram

9. Because of the higher probabilities assigned to the middle values of each variable the 100 billion cu. ft. size has the highest probability—4.35%. This number is calculated by multiplying the probabilities of each variable as follows: 0.29 × 0.50 × 0.60 × 0.50 = 0.0435. The 100 billion cu. ft. size is 36 times more probable than the largest size (.0435 ÷ .0012) = 36.

10. The average of the 27 field sizes is 129 billion cu. ft.

11. The risk-weighted size from the 27 probabilities is 29.25 billion cu. ft.—by design as much as by accident, near the risk-weighted values shown for the single case and the maximum-minimum cases.

12. We show two identical reserve sizes—70 billion cu. ft. Their make up comes from different values for net pay, recovery factor and land area. This coincidence should remind us that various combinations of these three parameters can produce similar reserves but with different probabilities of occurrence.

Things to Remember about Multiple Variables

You can quickly grasp the interrelation of our assumptions when viewing the probability estimates shown in Fig. 10–1.

For example, the initial probability assumption resulted from geologic judgments about wildcat risk—29% chance of a discovery. This number was introduced as a single value, but it also could be a variable. Consider the changes which would result on Fig. 10–1—all the final probabilities associated with a specific reserve size would change.

The more numerous the assumptions, the more numerous the cases. A computer must be used in complex cases, especially if you consider all of the economic variables which will be tacked onto these reserve estimates.

At this point you may want to throw up your hands and return to the simple case of three reserve sizes—maximum, minimum and most likely. Certainly there can be a point of diminishing return in regard to the number of cases. The number of cases required to define a prospect or problem is always a matter of judgment.

One point to remember for variables you want to test is three points define a curve, so test your key variables with three values for plotting purposes. Make sure the values cover as broad a range as you can reasonably envision—then all cases in between can be interpolated from graphs.

Finally since field sizes exhibit a lognormal distribution, prospect estimates logically should do likewise, and they do. See Fig. 10–2 for the plot of the 27 reserve sizes from Fig. 10–1. Nature warns us to ponder any field size distribution not lognormal. We can apply the same caution to prospect size estimates.

Cumulative Probability Distribution

Before we leave our complex situation of 27 cases, one other plot will be shown.

We can generate a cumulative probability distribution which will take into account the probability of a dry hole. Such a curve is shown in Fig. 10–3. It was constructed by rearranging the cases by size from the largest to the smallest and cumulating the probabilities.

With this curve we can determine the probability of finding reserve sizes throughout the range of the prospect's potential, as estimated from our judgments. The most likely size (or larger)

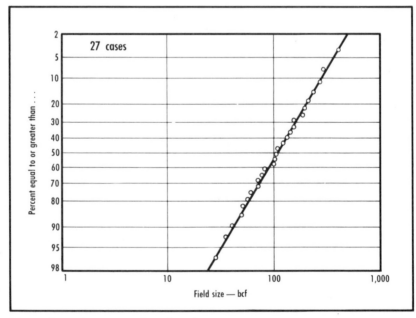

Fig. 10–2 Prospect size distribution

designated previously shows on this curve a chance of 12.5%. The probability of finding only half as much, 50 billion cu. ft., is 25%. Actually the cumulative probability curve demonstrates that we have a most likely range rather than a specific size. That range is the steepest part of the curve.

At the top of the graph a second scale is shown. It is the present value profit associated with these reserve sizes. From this scale the complete range of PVP is shown plus the probability of achieving a given profit. For example, we have a 12.5% chance of making $7.5 million (PVP at 10%), but a slim chance of 2.5% of making $15.0 million. This curve puts the expected value of $1.11 million in a better perspective. The full range of possible profit potential provides a better understanding of the School prospect.

Fig. 10–3 Cumulative probability distribution

Even More Complex

With computer programs available even more cases could be tried. The formula on p. 166 showed that the number of values raised to the power of the parameters gives the number of cases.

$$(\text{No. of Values})^{\text{No. Parameters}} \qquad\qquad (\text{Eq. 10–1})$$

Four values for 5 parameters would result in $(4)^5$ cases or 1024 cases. Such a number puts us well beyond the scope of this manual, which aims to teach without a computer. You also may be well beyond the scope of your data.

If, however, you desire a number of cases run based on a small amount of input, a technique is available. It is called Monte Carlo simulation.[2,3,4] Those interested in a simple explanation of the method are referred to Appendix D.

Time for Reflection

Does this chapter demonstrate too many calculations, methods and techniques for a subject with so few facts and such wide ranges of possibilities? Herein lies a significant point. The greater the risks and the more numerous the uncertainties, the less likely that one case or a few cases will adequately define the opportunity. When the range of possibilities is great, we do a disservice by supplying only one answer. It is equivalent to telling someone the next roll of the dice will total seven!

REVIEW

In this chapter applications of the concepts from the previous chapters were reviewed. No matter how many variables are tested, how many cases are run, ask this question, "Are you satisfied with the assumptions (probabilities)?" Do you agree with the range chosen for the critical variables? If so, then techniques are available to tell much of what can be known about these assumptions.

The range of possible answers to the profitability of an exploration investment is so broad that no single case can describe a prospect. Superior mathematical techniques do not eliminate the need for judgment, and even the most sophisticated techniques are limited by the accuracy of input. But risk analysis techniques can better enable the explorationist to understand his investment opportunity. They are one more tool in his arsenal of weapons in a field of such uncertainties that every tool is needed.

PROBLEMS

1. To test your understanding of expected value, solve this problem. (Review the steps in calculating expected value.) Someone offers to pay you $5 for every double six you roll if you give them 20¢ each for all other outcomes. Should you play? Answer by determining the expected value of each roll.

2. Take your favorite prospect. Select some basis for choosing several field sizes. Calculate a risk-weighted field size. Plot your prospect estimates on lognormal probability paper to see if they form a straight line. If you used the method shown in Fig. 10–1, plot a cumulative probability distribution as in Fig. 10–3.

BIBLIOGRAPHY

1. Grayson, C. Jackson, Jr. "Decisions Under Uncertainty," Harvard Business School, Boston, 1960, p. 236-250.
2. Jefferson, James T. "Risk Analysis Improves Pipeline Decisions," *Oil & Gas Journal*, August 31, 1970, p. 80.
3. Smith, Marvin B. "Estimate Reserves By Using Computer Simulation Method," *Oil & Gas Journal*, March 11, 1968, p. 81.
4. Hertz, D.B. "Risk Analysis in Capital Investment," Harvard Business Review, January-February 1964, p. 95-106.

11 Analysis, the Computer and You

No discussion of economic analysis would be complete without discussing the role of the computer in modern analysis technology. In the beginning, the basic usage of the computer was that of a "number cruncher"—a means of faster calculation. Today's computer usage is a far cry from the early beginnings of vacuum tubes and limited storage capacity and unimaginative output tables.

One of the early computers, the IBM 650, used vacuum tubes (and required several tons of air conditioning to keep it cool) and had a storage capacity of only 2,000 spaces. Furthermore, these spaces were on a revolving cylinder, not the type of random access we have today from "chips". The desktop computer now can do more than the early mainframe computers and with easier entry of data and much more useful and understandable output. Graphic output is now standard on most computer programs. The input is not long lines of carefully spaced numbers and symbols, but related to "menus" where you do little more than fill in the blanks.

All economic analysis is now performed by computers, much of it on desktop models. This remarkable change puts economic analysis into the hands of anyone who wants to take the time to learn a specific program. No programming languages are required, just a little time to learn an individual program. Commercial programs abound; however, many companies have written their own in-house programs. A company can often, for a fee, get the supplier of a commercial program to modify it for its specific purposes. Computer programs related to analysis come in varying degrees of complexity and price. A few brief programs sell for less than $100; others may cost tens of thousands of dollars and a few require a connection to a large computer (a mainframe connection).

Selecting Your Computer Program

With so many existing programs available, a company needs a strong justification for taking the time to write its own program. Even if you have programming skills available, there is a perpetual maintenance problem. Program changes can be necessitated by a variety of causes. Most frequently they are changes in either tax laws or state regulations. Sometimes intracompany requirements produce a need for a modification of the base program. Whatever the reasons, a maintenance demand goes with each in-house program. Often these must be met on extremely limited time commitments. If you use a commercially available program, the responsibility for all changes belongs to the firm selling the program. Furthermore, there are others using the program to detect errors (bugs) that might not be caught under your type of usage.

The following steps are useful in selecting a commercial program for your own use.

1. First, estimate your needs based on both current usage and possible usage in the next few years.
2. Select several programs that meet those needs.
3. Compare the programs relative to your needs.
   Is the program easy to use?
   How much training time is needed?
   How much input is required?
   How easily can default values be changed?
   Is the output as you desire it?
   If not, can it be modified easily?
   Does it have graphic capabilities?
   Does it have Monte Carlo or similar simulation?
   Can all variables be tested at high and low values?
   Will the manufacturer make small changes to meet your specific needs?
   Can the program be used on a microcomputer or does it require a mainframe connection?
4. Having answered all questions about each program, a comparison of cost versus desired features can be made and a selection made. When the final selection has been made, find a user of the program and check their satisfaction with the program and the seller of the program. An unfavorable report here may influence your decision.

5. Finally, before accepting any program, check its answers to one of your typical analyses either with another known program or with a hand calculation. Never accept a new program without checking against a known answer.

Not all commercial programs handle exploratory opportunities with equal ease. Most do, but make sure that the program chosen handles risk entries, exploration expenditures (separate from all other expenditures) and the timing of play expenditures as you wish them to be handled.

Sample Output From An Existing Program

With so many programs to choose from it is difficult to pick just one to illustrate a few samples of output. Nevertheless, the program chosen (with permission of the seller) is one issued by Intera Technologies of Austin, Texas[1]. The name of the program is GO! This program has one of the desirable features for an exploratory investment, the ability to enter low-side and high-side values. Furthermore, it produces a graphic plot of key values showing the full range of possible answers based on the high-, low- and best-estimate values entered.

A good starting point is Table 11–1 which gives the profitability summary for the GO! program. Note that minimum and maximum values are shown as well as the best estimate (which has been called the most-likely estimate in prior chapters). The summary shows payout and discounted payout for the three values. The discount rate used (12%) is listed at the bottom of the summary table. The present value profit (discounted at 12%) is shown along with five different rate of return yardsticks calculated. The net present value shown excludes the investment. All have been discussed in prior chapters except the sinking fund rate of return, which is not often used for exploratory investments.

Table 11–2 shows the cash flow and discounted cash flow for the three cases. Similar tabular output exists for total revenue, total costs, production, tangible and intangible costs, total capital costs, exploratory expenditures, operating costs, income taxes, state and local taxes, windfall profit taxes, total taxes, etc. Many computer programs have a final summary showing all costs and expenses by years for a single case. You may prefer this type of output. GO! is oriented to those who wish to use its simulator to demonstrate the effect of uncertainties in key variables.

11:54am   G O ? PROFITABILITY SUMMARY

| | 95% CONFIDENCE INTERVAL | | |
PROFITABILITY MEASURES	MINIMUM	BEST ESTIMATE	MAXIMUM
Payout (Years)............... :	5.64	6.07	6.46
* Discounted Payout (Years)....:	5.91	6.44	6.98
* Net Present Value (x $1000)..:	9939.30	12764.05	17020.17
* Present Value Profit (x $1000):	4257.24	7082.00	11338.12
* Internal Rate of Return (%)..:	32.58	42.03	54.14
* Modified Rate of Return (%)..:	21.17	25.23	30.39
** Growth Rate of Return (%)...:	16.25	18.14	20.50
** Sinking Fund Rate of Return (%):	23.00	30.30	41.30
* Percentage Gain on Investment (%):	11.00	18.30	29.30

* Discount Rate = 12.0 %/Annum

F1 Help

Table 11-1

11:57am   G O ↑   AFTER TAX CASH FLOW (x $1000)

all rows shown   columns 3 to 4 of 4

YEAR	Cash Flow			Discounted Cash Flow		
	Minimum	Best Est.	Maximum	Minimum	Best Est.	Maximum
1985	-500.0	-500.0	-500.0	-472.5	-472.5	-472.5
1986	-823.0	-823.0	-823.0	-694.3	-694.3	-694.3
1987	-256.5	-256.5	-256.5	-193.2	-193.2	-193.2
1988	-1704.3	-1704.2	-1704.3	-1146.2	-1146.2	-1146.2
1989	-1633.6	-998.9	-219.5	-981.0	-599.8	-131.0
1990	-3234.8	4017.3	4971.7	-1734.4	2153.9	2665.7
1991	3873.5	4819.0	5970.2	1854.3	2307.0	2858.1
1992	3251.3	4128.0	5250.1	1389.7	1764.8	2244.0
1993	2519.1	3274.6	4330.8	961.4	1249.7	1652.1
1994	1638.9	2214.4	3083.1	558.5	754.5	1050.5
1995	1354.7	1878.5	2724.0	412.2	571.5	828.8
1996	1133.8	1616.7	2423.1	308.0	439.2	658.2
1997	976.4	1451.8	2237.2	236.0	352.1	542.6
1998	905.1	1406.6	2225.3	196.0	304.6	481.9
1999	926.7	1504.0	2439.6	179.2	296.8	471.7

↑more

F1 Help screen

Table 11–2

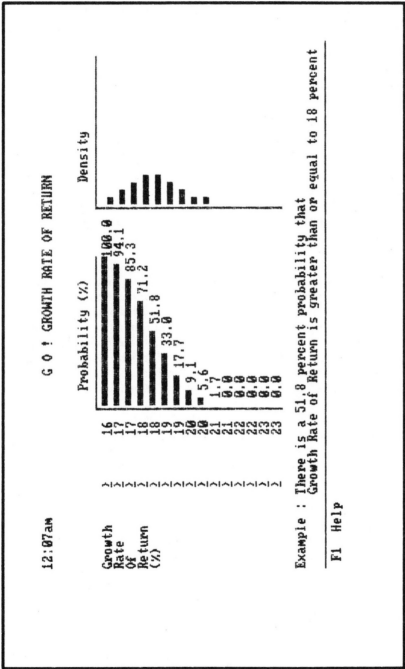

Fig. 11-1   Distribution of possible answers

GO! also provides the ability to show graphically the range of possibilities for key parameters developed from the three cases. Fig. 11–1 illustrates the distribution of possible answers for the Growth Rate of Return yardstick. If you comprehend variables better in graphic form and wish to see the full spectrum of possibilities, the figures generated by GO! will be useful.

REVIEW

No one today would dream of making a hand calculation for an economic analysis, just as no traveler wants an open cockpit, single-engine airplane for travel to distant cities. Yet the manual calculations required to complete the programs in this book do much to take the mystery from economic analysis. It pays to do a few simple hand calculations to comprehend what the algorithms in a computer program do with your data. No one needs to discount a cash flow, but until you have discounted a simple example, you may not know what values are plotted on a graph of present values to get the discounted cash flow rate. The computer has simplified all economic analyses in terms of quick answers and limited the amount of manpower tied up in calculations, per se. The computer has not replaced judgment, nor does it reduce risk. It is a valuable tool and because of its rapid calculation and graphic capability, it allows management an opportunity for a more complete review of the investment opportunities available.

The comments regarding computers, as in all other aspects of economic analysis in this textbook, are introductory in nature. An entire volume could be written on computer usage in economic analysis—well beyond the scope of this text.

The computer and the microcomputer in particular make life easier for the analyst. They shorten the timeframe for getting answers, but alas, they also markedly increase the kinds of questions asked. Vital to today's analysts, they are both boon and bane. Yet we would not want to do without them. No one wants to go back to the days of the desk calculator.

BIBLIOGRAPHY

1. Pahwa, Suresh, B., et. al., "Microcomputers Aid Investment Decisions," *Oil & Gas Journal*, Feb. 11, 1985.

12 Setting up an Exploration Evaluation

The final chapter will deal with the mechanics of setting up an evaluation of an exploratory opportunity. The minimum quantity of data will be reviewed, and its arrangement suggested with some comments on data quality. More than the most likely case will be considered. The most likely case is a useful tool, particularly in engineering economics, where the probabilities have narrower ranges, but in exploratory investments the range of possible answers is usually so broad it lessens the value of a single case.

Almost every exploratory opportunity is unique in certain respects. Therefore, our suggestions on data gathering, data format, evaluation methods and risk analysis do not preclude more specific techniques for any single opportunity. Perhaps the most common decision in exploration involves the prospect evaluation. It shall be used as our starting point. We shall refer to Chapters 5, 6, 7, 9, and 10 when the techniques used have been explained previously.

Gathering the Data

Our data gathering will begin with the prospect and expand beyond into a play or series of plays.

The gathering of data involves judgments at many points. The most knowledgeable explorationist should assist in the data accumulation to ensure quality and to enable him to influence judgments requiring exploratory experience. Place the same value on the input that will be placed on the output keeping in mind, of course, that some variables are more critical than others.

Fig. 12–1 Exploration Prospect Evaluation

Prospect name _____ Location _____ Date_____

BASIC EXPLORATION

Total acres in prospect _____ ; your net acres_____

Lease bonus–$/acre____; annual rental–$/acre____; royalty____

Geological effort–months____; geophysical effort–months & $____

Other exploration effort–$ _____

(Test wells, core drilling, overhead, etc.)

Composite risk factor (or success rate)–% _____

WELL DATA

No. wildcats to evaluate prospect ___; depth ___; your W.I. ____

Successful wildcat–$: tangible _____ ; Intangible _____

Dry wildcat–$_____ ; well spacing–acres _____

Successful development well–$: tangible_____; Intangible _____

Dry development well–$____; development drilling success
rate–% _____

Operating costs–$/completion/year_____

TIMING: Calendar Year(s)

Year of sale of production_____

Leasing_____ ; Geology & geophysics _____ ; drill wildcat(s) _____

Development well schedule–wells _____ _____ _____ _____ _____

year _____ _____ _____ _____ _____

RESERVES (If more than one zone, use separate sheet.)

Pay zone name_____ Oil or gas____ (If both: ratio of gas cap to oil
zone____)

(If gas: inert gas % _____ ; condensate–bbl/$\overline{\text{M}}$cf_____)

Productive acres: total _____ ; your acreage _____ ; depth _____

Average net pay–ft._____; recoverable reserves/acre-ft._____

Allowable_____; secondary recovery_____

REQUEST

Type evaluation desired (variables to be tested) _____

_____

Remarks_____

_____

_____

Date needed_____ Requested by _____

Fig. 12–1 shows the basic data needed for a prospect evaluation.
The data are segregated into four categories each of which will be
briefly discussed.

Basic Exploration

The beginning statistics deal with acreage. How large is the prospect in acres?

How much do you own? What was paid per acre, or is expected to be paid on acreage as yet not acquired? List the rental conditions and royalty considerations. All other exploratory data, the physical units and their corresponding costs, should be tabulated and related to time, i.e., in what year was the money spent. Some years may be future ones.

If you have not calculated a composite risk factor (and many analysts do not), what success rate (in per cent) is anticipated for this trend? Is it applicable to this prospect?

Remember that some of your data will represent capitalized costs and other data expensed items.

Well Data

Statistics about both wildcat and development wells need documentation.

Will more than one wildcat be needed to test the prospect? How deep? What is your working interest? Separate all well cost estimates into tangible and intangible segments. If a dry wildcat will cost less than a successful one (and it usually does), show its cost. What well spacing do you expect? How many successful and dry development wells will it take to develop the prospect and what is their cost? The direct operating costs associated with production should be recorded as well as indirect costs and overhead gleaned from appropriate accounting records.

Timing

Review Tables 5–1 and 5–2 for a reference on timing. Because we will discount future expenditures and revenue, timing is important. Consider carefully the scheduling of exploration expenditures and the drilling of development wells. The normal temptation in prospect evaluations is to over optimize the scheduling of exploratory expenditures and the rate of field development. Events can and often do alter our rate of exploration and field development. To expect everything to come off smoothly ignores a lot of painful history. Be realistic in timing. If in doubt make timing one of your variables.

Reserves

In view of all that's been said, the reserve data requested may seem skimpy.

It is. What is shown is absolutely minimal and would apply only for a most likely reserve estimate. Are you exploring in a mature trend? Do you have access to a field size distribution; if so, it is your starting point. Whatever reserve sizes you select, the field sizes should fit a lognormal distribution as outlined in Chapter 9. In prorated states the allowable is necessary information. For gas wells the rate of take (DCQ) must be estimated. Allowables and takes must often be related to knowledge about reservoir characteristics. Is the formation of such low permeability that deliverability is limited? Special field problems must also be noted; examples would be: high per cent of inert gas, CO_2 perhaps; presence of H_2S; remoteness from market; unusual shrinkage, and so forth. The data category on reserves could obviously be expanded; just how much will depend a lot on your data base and whether you have access to a computer.

The most reasonable expansion of the reserve data shown would be the inclusion of a minimum size and a maximum size. Both sizes should be realistic and be equivalent in size to the 90th percentile (low side) and 10th percentile (high side)—as would be shown on lognormal probability paper.[1]

Defining the Request

The type of analysis needed must be carefully considered. Both the requester and analyst should participate in defining the request. In areas where a single factor (reserves, bonus per acre, success rate, etc.) cannot be stipulated, some sensitivity testing should be undertaken. Begin by asking, "What do we want to know about this prospect?"

Are you trying to determine what bonus you can pay? If so, set up several cases to check various bonus prices which can be paid. Other variables can be tested by varying the reserve size, success rate, etc. Are risks quantified or at least tested for their impact on potential profits?

The definition of a request is a key step. When the important factors are carefully reviewed, the result is a well-defined evaluation and fewer recalculations.

Sensitivity Testing

Some comments have already have been made on sensitivity tests. In general you should test the sensitivity of any factor recognized as critical. A critical factor is one in which a possible change makes a significant change in profits or guideline yardsticks.

We can demonstrate a few factors using the School prospect. In Table 12–1 the sensitivity of several changes on yardsticks of the School prospect is noted:

TABLE 12–1

Sensitivity Checks, School Prospect

Case No.	Case Basis	AVP, $M	PVP @ 10%	DCFR %
1	Base Case	6,998	2,254	24.5
2	Double Expl. Expend.	4,675	385	11.9
3	Double Dev. Expend.	4,529	607	14.1
4	2-Yr Revenue Delay	6,998	1,232	16.2

From these simple illustrations, the most significant variables can be inferred. Case 1 is the base case used in prior chapters for the School prospect. At this point in the book the numbers for AVP, PVP @ 10% and the DCFR should be familiar.

A critical variable in any exploratory evaluation is the amount of money spent in exploration. Case 2 in Table 12–1 shows the results of doubling the exploration expenditures. (In a sense, you can think of this as halving the success rate.) Spending twice the scheduled amount in finding the School prospect reduces the total money received (the AVP) to $4.675 million. The PVP at 10% is sharply reduced—to $385,000. The DCFR is reduced from 24.5% for the base case to 11.9% for the case of double exploration expenditures.

Notice the effect of doubling the development expenditures, Case 3. The AVP is about the same as doubling the exploration expenditures, $4.53 million. However, because the development investments take place later in the cash flow stream, and are thus discounted more, time value yardsticks are affected less. The present value profit at 10% is $607,000, larger than for the doubling of exploratory expenditures, and the DCFR is 14.1%. A delayed expenditure is not as harmful as a current one—something for the explorationist to remember. His expenditures are always up front.

In Case 4, the effect of a two-year delay in revenue is shown. The two-year delay was accomplished by moving the income stream two years into the future, beginning in year six instead of year four. The AVP is the same as for the base case. No additional money was spent. We get our money later, however, and the time value yardsticks reflect the low. The PVP at 10% is reduced from $2.254 million to $1.232 million; and the DCFR is decreased from 24.5% to 16.2%. Delays in revenue cost money because you don't have the annual cash flows to reinvest.

Inflation—A Form of Sensitivity Testing

In any cash flow analysis the question arises as to how to treat inflation. In times of modest inflation, no more than two or four percent per year, inflation can almost be ignored. Why? It gets swamped by the more critical parameters such as risk or reserve size. However, at higher rates of inflation, greater than six percent, it should be considered.

Opinions on how to handle inflation differ. They center around three approaches as follows:

1. *Constant dollar method.* In the constant dollar approach the projections of the various components of cash flow are expressed as dollars of the year in which the evaluation or analysis is made. This method assumes that prices and costs will inflate at the same rate and thus offset each other—at least approximately. In effect, you are ignoring inflation in using this method, if your assumption is not valid.

2. *Component inflation method.* In the component inflation method the inflation rate for each cost or price component in the cash flow stream is forecast independently. For example, you may feel wages will increase at 6% per year during the life of your investment but that material cost will increase at 10% per year. If so, you take the wage-related costs and increase them at 6% per year. Material costs are increased at the higher rate. Using this method you apply your best knowledge to each component of the cash flow stream. Thus wellhead prices for oil and gas, drilling costs, lease and well expense, leasing costs, etc. can be forecast based on recent experience or reasonable future expectations.

3. *The single inflation rate method.* This method applies a single rate of inflation to all cost (or price) ingredients. The assumption precludes individual component rates. It would apply where you feel data insufficient to develop realistic or accurate rates of inflation for individual components of cash flow.

Some analysts go one step further. They say, in effect: "All this inflation forecasting is fine—but in 1990 when the cash flow stream returns $100,000, that sum will not buy as much as $100,000 today!" Thus a "deflator" is advocated to correct future dollars to what they would buy today. Even this criticism does not apply in all cases. It would probably be more appropriate for drilling costs, but certainly not so for rapidly changing technology—small electronic calculators being the prime example of a decreasing cost item, not an inflating one.

So what do you do? None of these methods promises absolute accuracy. All involve key assumptions about the future. If you think you have good information on a few parts of the cash flow stream, you may favor the component method. You can throw up your hands and inflate not at all, or use a single escalation factor. You have to choose according to what you believe will provide the most realistic answer— the one which will enable you to best optimize your investment policy for the long pull. However, if the rate of inflation approaches double digits you need to take it into account.

The Critical Variables

For most exploration investments, the significant variables are:

1. Risk.
2. Amount of exploratory expenditures.
3. Field size—reserves per well.
4. Deliverability (especially for gas discoveries).
5. Delay in revenue.
6. Wellhead price.

Each of these variables will be discussed briefly. No specifics will be given because of the unique characteristics of each prospect, plus the special conditions associated with the hostile environments of Alaska and offshore. In offshore environments where development, facility and producing costs are large, these costs become important economic parameters. The six variables we have listed would be critical to any exploratory investment whether onshore or offshore.

Risk

The investment cash flow in Table 5–2 for the School prospect assumes at least one, possibly two, dry wildcats. In making this assumption, we are departing a bit from a normal one-well-on-a-structure evaluation. It is done for illustration purposes. The methodology recommended here is just as applicable if only one well per prospect is assumed. Assuming that two dry wells were drilled, then the play resulting in the successful School prospect had a success rate of 33%, slightly above the calculated wildcat risk. In Table 12–1, Case 2, doubling the exploratory expenditures without doubling the revenue is about equivalent to halving the success rate—say to 17%. We see then that the DCFR of the School prospect is very sensitive to "risk" changes. Furthermore, to achieve a 10% DCFR will require almost a 15% success rate, assuming we have a large number of similar plays.

Whatever basic data are available to measure risk, it is one of the key variables. Consider it carefully and check the effect of various risk values on your prospect's cash flow. One simple method to measure

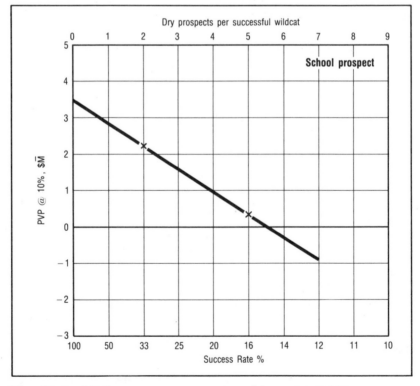

Fig. 12–2 Minimum success rate to achieve 10% DCFR

the effect of risk is a plot of PVP at your desired minimum discount rate versus the number of dry prospects per successful prospect. The use of dry prospects per successful wildcat produces a straight line on your graph so only two points are needed. With a computer three points are just as easily obtained as two and will verify your line.

Fig. 12–2 has such a plot for the School prospect. The two points for the graph are PVPs for the base Case 1, and the doubling of exploration expense—representing two dry prospects and five dry prospects per producer, respectively. The straight line was extended to the Y axis and to the zero PVP line. The present value profit at 10% becomes zero at 5.5 dry prospects per success so the limiting success rate is:

$$\frac{1}{5.5 \; + \; 1} \; \times \; 100 \; = \; 15.4\%$$

(The successful wildcat divided by the dry wildcats plus the successful one times 100 equals the success rate.) This per cent is somewhat theoretical. You might not have enough prospects in the play (like the School prospect) to test such a success rate. The value lies in the limit. Suppose the minimum permissible success rate is two or three per cent and that your experience in the trend has been substantially higher (say 25 or 33%): then you can feel reasonably confident that your prospect is not limited by economic yardsticks or the other assumptions from which you calculated the 2% limit. One other point comes from Fig. 12–2. The intersection with the Y axis is the PVP with no dry prospects, or 100% success. The PVP at 10% for this case is $3.5 million.

Another graphic form to obtain the minimum success rate involves a graphic plot of the risk-weighting of an individual prospect. Shown in Fig. 12–3 it requires the AFIT cost (PVP at 10%) of a dry venture (in this case—$200,000) and the results of a successful prospect—$620,000.

The plot for Bearcreek prospect shows that a 25% chance of success is required to achieve a zero PVP at 10%. It then is the minimum allowable success rate. You can see graphically that any smaller success rate would necessitate a higher PVP at 10% (in effect a larger prospect). On the other hand a guaranteed higher success rate, say 50%, would require less PVP from a successful prospect—in effect a smaller prospect.

Variations of this chart can serve as graphical solutions to problems similar to those depicted by a payoff table. Suppose for

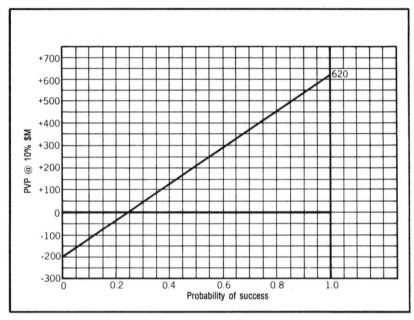

Fig. 12–3   Minimum success rate at 10% PVP, Bearcreek prospect

example that you thought the chances of a 25% success rate were questionable. Suppose further you calculate that a farmout with favorable retained royalty would yield $300,000 from a successful prospect. What success rate would you need to have before it is worth taking the risk of a working interest? Remember that in a farmout you have zero money at risk, zero PVP at 10%.

The solution is shown in Fig. 12–4. The farmout line crosses the working interest line at 40%. Thus, you would need a success rate greater than 40% for the working interest venture to give you a better profit than the farmout. You are assuming that your probability risking is accurate, of course. However, if the 25% estimate leaves you uncomfortable the answer is farmout.

Graphic solutions sometimes offer simple pictorial explanations for analytical problems.

Exploration Expenditures

The comparison of Case 2 to Case 1 in Table 12–1 demonstrates the significance of exploratory expenditures to time value yardsticks.

Remember that exploratory investments start at the front end of

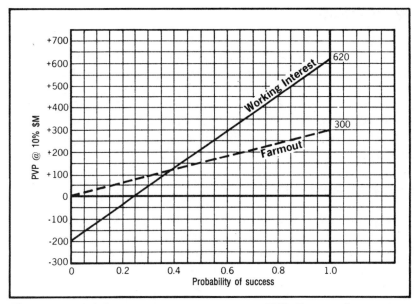

Fig. 12–4   Minimum success rate at 10% PVP, Bearcreek prospect

the cash flow stream and are discounted very little. As such a dollar of exploratory expenditures is more significant than a dollar of development expenditures, the latter is farther down the cash flow stream. Comparing Case 3 to Case 2 in Table 12–1 shows this relationship clearly. The AVP is about the same for both cases, but because the development expenditures are later (discounted more) a difference exists in their effect on time value yardsticks.

Field Size and Reserves Per Well

The total quantity of reserves found is important, particularly if the exploratory expenditures are large.

The recovery per well is equally important. Once sufficient reserves are produced to overcome the effect of exploratory cost, the DCFR will approach that of the average development well. Obviously, the DCFR for a prospect cannot exceed that of the average of the development wells. This last statement has special meaning for high cost areas. You may have a trillion cu.-ft.-gas field, but if it is deep (say 25,000 ft.) and you can only produce one billion cu. ft. per well, it is uneconomic. The reserves per well are important.

Deliverability

Closely related to recovery per well is the actual rate of flow from an oil or gas well. By now you realize that any factor which lengthens payout lowers the DCFR. One way to lengthen payout is to have a well with a very low production rate. Since most oil wells are shallow with attendant lower investments, deliverability is more critical with deep gas wells. A deep gas well needs a high flow rate for profitability. If you face low permeability at depth and thus low producing rates, you have a very critical parameter.

Delay in Revenue

Case 4, Table 12–1, illustrates the effect of delay in revenue on present value yardsticks. Delay can come about from mechanical well problems, a slow development rate for the field, restricted market outlets, awaiting construction of complex lease facilities or a pipeline and so forth. The more delay the longer the payout (at least on the exploratory investment) and the lower the DCFR.

Delay is one factor over which the explorationist often has no control. Nevertheless, if in doubt check the sensitivity of yardsticks to possible delays. Not to do so would be to fail to describe the uncertainties of the opportunity.

Needless to say, you can do a lot more checking of sensitivities with a computer available. With practice and experience, however, one can spot almost by inspection the variables which need testing for sensitivity. Some factors not mentioned would be critical in different evaluations. A partial analysis of a downstream investment might have costs critical to profits. In exploratory investments, the costs of exploration precede other investments by such a time margin that they are much more critical. For this reason the experienced analyst spends more time and care on the exploratory phase of his investment stream than on other downstream investments. The importance of timing on yardsticks requires it!

A delay in both revenue and investment of the same time period will not change the DCFR. However, it will lower the PVP for all discount rates below the DCFR. In the case of the School prospect, for example, the effects of delay (both revenue and investment, remember) are shown in Table 12–2.

The graphic expression in loss of discounted profit is shown in Fig. 12–5. The lower PVP with delay clearly shows one of the

TABLE 12–2

The Effect of Delay on Present Value
School Prospect
(Thousands of Dollars)

	Delay, years		
	0	5	10
AVP	6,998	6,998	6,998
Discounted Profit			
−10%	2,254	1,428	927
−20%	436	174	70

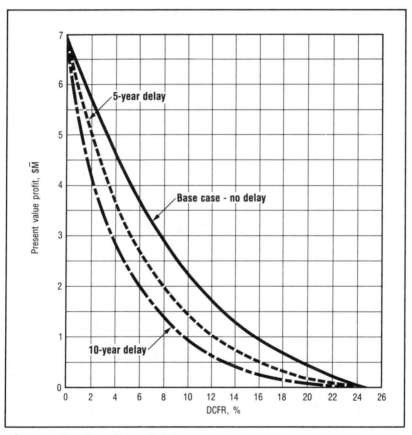

Fig. 12–5 The effect of delay on present value, School prospect

weaknesses of using only DCFR as the yardstick. As we have said, there is no perfect single yardstick.

Price

In the first edition of *Exploration Economics* price was not listed as a critical variable. It has become a most critical variable because of the large increases in inflation since 1973. In the regulated prices of the 1970s, low values often precluded further field development for both "old" oil and interstate natural gas. Furthermore, inflation was always two jumps ahead of regulatory bodies' ability to react to the need for price changes.

The Natural Gas Policy Act of 1978 intended to provide for the orderly deregulation of much of the natural gas supply. In so doing it added much confusion. There were from 15 to 20 categories of gas, each with its own price schedule. And for the first time gas sold intrastate came under Federal price control. Thus, with intended decontrol came more control.

The deregulation of crude oil prices in the 1980s came at a time when prices were approaching their highest levels in decades. In fact, the prices of the early 1980s were the highest sustained levels in the history of the petroleum industry. The boom, as we reviewed earlier, was followed by a most rapid collapse in price.

Price is a key variable. The wide swings in price levels of the 1980s proved this point beyond any doubts. In today's analyses, every prospect should be tested against several price forecasts, with particular emphasis on the low-range forecast. Would you be willing to make the investment if the low-range forecast became reality? It is an important question to ask. Don't forget a natural gas or oil price change can occur after you have already made your investment. So test the sensitivity to various price assumptions. Then make your best judgment.

Play vs. Basin Risk

If you work for a large company, a plot similar to Fig. 12–2 can be useful. The successful exploration program must carry the unsuccessful ones, a fact overlooked by many of our critics. If you wish to check the "carrying" ability of a successful play, plot PVP, at your guideline discount rate, versus dry plays per successful one. The number of dry plays your successful one could carry occurs where the line crosses zero PVP.

The best method for prospect appraisal is still to establish a chance of success for the prospect as outlined in Chapter 9. The "carrying" concept is easily understood, but the individual probability for each prospect allows aggregations of prospects or plays. It gives the same answer as the carrying concept, but is a much more useful number for additional applications. It is the basis for risk-weighting.[2]

The Economics of New Basins

One of the most baffling problems facing the explorationist deals with the economic results from exploration in virgin basins.

Where no oil or gas has been found, the facts are few. This type of evaluation is more geologic than economic. The assumptions made concerning the presence or absence of hydrocarbons, depth and type of reserve and field size will normally outweigh all other input factors in the effect on economic yardsticks.

What, then, can the analyst contribute that will assist in the decision? He can show the results of a proposed exploration program and determine the magnitude of reserves required to make a profit from these investments. If the basic assumptions do not produce desired yardstick levels they can be re-examined. Changes may produce different yardstick levels. If no changes are felt possible or necessary, then poor economic results suggest caution. A different level of expenditures can be planned.

In summary, then, an evaluation of a program in a virgin basin can only show the economic results of assumed reserves and risks and proposed expenditures. If the field size and number to support the program appear reasonable, proceed. If your most reasonable assumptions do not produce profitable results, the warning flag is out.

Another Sensitivity Check

If you wish to illustrate sensitivities graphically, a common means is by use of a spider diagram. These diagrams have been shown in evaluation literature for many years.

In Fig. 12–6 a sample of such a sensitivity chart is plotted. The ordinate is present value profit (PVP) at the desired discount rate. The abscissa shows the base case at 1.0 and deviations from the base case. To the right parameter values are greater than the base case, to the left smaller. The base case parameters are:

30 BCF Prospect
1.0 $\overline{\text{Mcf}}$/D Initial Potential (IP)
$1/_6$ Royalty
50% Success Rate
$25 Per Acre Bonus

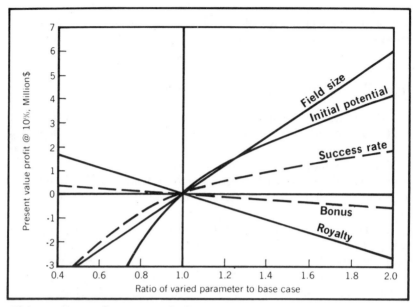

Fig. 12–6 Profit vs. varied parameter

Each parameter must be varied at least twice to get a curve—one value above and one below the base case.

Sensitivities are indicated by the curves drawn on the chart. All curves pass through the ratio of 1.0 since it is the starting point for either plus or minus deviations. Thus, Fig. 12–6 shows how field size, initial potential, success rate, bonus and royalty vary from the base case but only *if all other values remain constant*. The last phrase is important. The curve indicated for initial potential shows changes in PVP at 10% for that parameter alone, with all other parameters remaining at the base case value. Therefore, one of the limitations of spider diagrams is that they test only one parameter at a time.

There are other parameters not tested. Examples are well cost, operating cost, wellhead price, etc. The choice of which parameters to evaluate must come from the analyst. Those chosen should be only the factors in which small variations make large changes in profits.

Spider diagrams allow useful comparisons. For example, suppose you had to give a one-third royalty instead of one-sixth. Looking toward the right side of the chart, one-third royalty is equal to a ratio of 2.0 relative to the base case value. You can see that the PVP at 10% is a loss of almost $3 million if the royalty goes to one-third. Note also that to compensate for such a high royalty it would require 1.6 times the base case initial potential or 1.5 times the field size. In this sense, spider diagrams can compare two variables simultaneously showing what positive effect could overcome the negative effect on profits caused by other factors. A spider diagram is a sort of trade-off chart because of the ability to compare changing parameters to a base case.

Choosing the base case is important. Normally it should be at the lower end of field size so as to check marginality. A base case could be chosen so that the PVP at 10% would be zero.

In the particular instance shown, the bonus per acre, in the range expected, is not a critical factor and could be eliminated from the graph. The greater the slope of a curve the more significant the variable is to the project. Again, the significance of the base case is illustrated. A base case of $500 per acre would generate a bonus curve with much greater slope.

Spider diagrams demonstrate the profitable limits of parameters when the PVP becomes zero. In the example shown in Figure 12–6 the base case was chosen to coincide with zero PVP at 10%. Thus, lines below zero denote negative effects on profits, those above positive effects. For example, lower bonus and royalty produce greater profits than the base case. Conversely, higher bonus and royalty reduce profits. Larger field size, IP, and higher success rates increase present value profits. Lower values for each parameter reduce profits.

How can you use this diagram as a trade-off chart? You use it in this manner—balancing a negative effect on profits to an equal positive effect. For example, what does it take to offset an increase in royalty to one-fourth (a ratio of 1.5 relative to the base case)? At 1.5, the negative effect of increasing royalty to one-fourth is about $1.5 million (PVP at 10%). To offset this loss requires an increase in IP to 1.25 times the base or 1.25 million cubic feet per day. Therefore, if the sum of the negative and positive effects equals zero, the changes in the two parameters equal a trade-off.

Spider diagrams have limitations:

1. They are related to a single case from which each variable is increased or decreased in value.
2. You must choose the right parameters to vary.
3. The number of cases needed to build a spider diagram usually requires access to a computer—not a serious limitation to most explorationists.

Spider diagrams do not have to be constructed so that the base case has a present value profit of zero. It is advisable that a negative

PVP can be shown for each parameter to enable easy trade-off comparisons. A base case near zero PVP would suffice almost as well as the example shown.

Spider diagrams test sensitivity in a unique way and allow a visual representation of the trade-offs between parameters. If you have access to a computer you may find this representation valuable. You can always draw more than one spider diagram if you wish to test more than one base case.

Using FSD Curves When Discovery Size is Decreasing

Many economists and mathematicians in dealing with a finite number of fields would prefer analyses which recognize "sampling without replacement." In other words, does your analysis take into account the fact that each new field found subtracts one from the total available to be found? The math for sampling without replacement is not unduly complex, but one can handle the problem with adequate accuracy by means of shifting field size distributions (FSD).

In Fig. 12–7 several FSDs are shown. Each is designated by a lower case letter. Curve b is the entire population of fields to date. It represents all of the fields discovered in the Great Gulch Basin from the first year of discovery to the present. Curve a represents the FSD for fields found in the first decade of basin life. In an active basin with 40 to 50 years of history, you may want to plot several decade curves.

Note the larger size of fields in the beginning. The median (50th percentile point) for curve a is 20 million barrels. For the entire history of the basin (curve b) the median size is only 10 million barrels. Obviously, the more recent discoveries have been smaller. Sure enough, curve c shows that for the most recent decade the median has slipped to 5.2 million barrels. Discoveries are getting smaller in the Great Gulch Basin and the analyst must recognize this change. How? The way to do this is to estimate curve d—a projection of a future distribution covering the period of the next decade.

Curve d will not be absolutely accurate (as with most forecasts), but it does move in the right direction. Until new fields are discovered to disprove the slope, assume that curve d will have the same general slope as curves a, b and c. You estimate curve d by plotting the median size versus time (actually the midpoint of a time period) then projecting the median size into the future. Put that median point on the graph and draw a line parallel to curves a, b and c. One thing you do know—this method is better than using curve c, b or a if you are

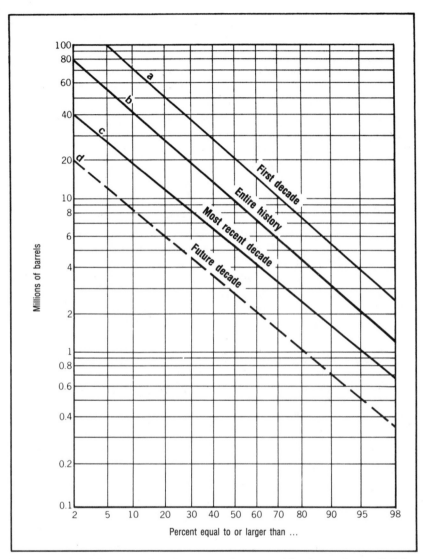

Fig. 12–7 Field size distributions change with time, Great Gulch Basin

looking for the same type of prospect or objective. New technology or a new play could of course cause a new wave of larger discoveries. It may be a deeper pay or a newly recognized objective. The method just described is ideal when you have assumed you are essentially continuing an existing play. However, if a new play in the basin changes the discovery sizes, the new information will help you draw a new curve. The importance of this graph is to give you a basis for showing what you expect your discovery size to be. It shows you have given some thought to "sampling without replacement."

Before we leave this rough method for sampling without replacement a few comments. Curve b represents the entire basin; it is all the history on sizes. Curves a and c are subsets of b. They represent portions of b and would have fewer fields involved. As such, from a practical viewpoint they might not yield as good a lognormal plot. However, if the sample is large enough, even subsets will yield reasonable lognormal fits.

Having projected the future field size distribution and knowing the average success rate you analyze a sample of fields (or if only one, the median) to see if you can make money from the fields associated with the new (future) distribution. By this method you will answer in a logical manner, the question "can you make money from the decreasing size of future discoveries." You also determine when to get out of a play that no longer provides discoveries of sufficient size to yield acceptable profits.

Review of Evaluation Procedures

At this point we have completed the evaluation of the School prospect, having carried it from a lead to a discovery. As a final review for the chapter, a sequence of steps is outlined for prospect or play evaluations with the appropriate reference to prior chapters.

1. Gather pertinent data with the aim of building the investment cash flow and income cash flow.
2. Separate exploratory and development investments into categories shown in Table 5–5. Then build the investment cash flow stream, Table 5–6.
3. From regulatory rules establish the flow rate per well and for the field. Consult a reservoir engineer for the advice on the proper flow based on reservoir characteristics. From crude or gas price, calculate annual revenue and following the steps in Tables 5–3 and 5–4 calculate the income cash flow.
4. Combine investment and income cash flows to get net cash flow (AFIT).
5. Adjust cash flow for sensitivity tests desired and discount base case and adjusted cash flows.

6. Consider risk by the payoff table, success rate or whatever method best describes your investment opportunity.
7. Calculate yardsticks as outlined in Chapter 7. Show from the sensitivity and risk calculations the change in yardsticks caused by critical parameters.
8. If satisifed with the economic and geologic description of the opportunity, make a recommendation or decision.

A word of caution. When dealing in prospect evaluation, the decision point, year zero, occurs after some funds have been spent. Frequently, these prior expenditures are excluded because the decision point is *now*. However, each prospect must bear its proportionate share of all exploratory costs—otherwise you would never fully account for all costs. One can raise the guideline DCFR a few points higher to compensate; or if the average prospect shows a DCFR well above the minimum guideline, ignore prior costs but remember that the actual rate of return is less than stated.

EPILOGUE

The time has come to ascertain if the goals at the outset have been reached. The reader is the best judge. In a primer, one must deal, purposely, somewhat behind the state of the art. The principles and procedures included are considered necessary as the footstool to further investigation.

No evaluation technique has been intended to be shown as absolute or final. History demonstrates continuous evolution of techniques and today's techniques are part of this continuing evolution. The literature of today reflects efforts toward further refinement of existing techniques as well as a few new ideas; and the literature is always behind the state of the art, particularly that from the larger companies.

No apology is given to the expert for the generalization necessary. In the beginning one must state positively a few ideas which should later be qualified to some extent. This book is no exception.

If a new idea or two from this book helps you understand the next evaluation, or if you feel able to discuss exploration investment evaluations more easily and intelligently, then the efforts have been worthwhile and the goals set forth have been achieved.

PROBLEMS

1. Using the cash flow streams for the School prospect from Chapter 5, calculate the reduction in PVP @ 10% caused by doubling the exploratory expenditures (years 0 through 3).
2. Prove that doubling the development investment has less effect than a corresponding change in exploratory investment.
3. Illustrate the effect of a two-year delay in revenue for the School prospect.
4. Illustrate a graphic solution for DCFR from discounted present values in Problem 2, case 3 (See Table 12–1).
5. South Florida Option

   You own a 50% W.I. in acreage in South Florida and are approached by an operator to participate in the drilling of a well. Another alternative is to farmout to the operator and keep a $^1/_{16}$ override, convertible to a 50% W.I. at payout.

The unrisked well economics for the two options are:

	50% W.I. Partner	You Farmout
AVP, $M	278	147
PVP @ 14%, $M	117	78

a. With a cost of capital at 14%, should you join or farmout if you think there is a 30% chance of success? —If you join, you risk 50% of a dry hole at $150M BFIT, or $75M AFIT.
b. What success rate do you need to have before the W.I. gives you a better PVP at 14% than a farmout?

BIBLIOGRAPHY

1. Megill, Robert E., *An Introduction to Risk Analysis, 2 ed.* PennWell Books, 1984, Chapter 16.
2. Megill, Robert E., "Prospect Appraisal: The Best Method," AAPG *Explorer*, Feb. 1985.

Appendix A

TABLE 1

Summary of Allowables
State of Texas

Depth	1947 Depth yardstick b/d				1965 Depth yardstick b/d					NPX	Marg. all.
	10 Ac.	20 Ac.	40 Ac.	80 Ac.	10 Ac.	20 Ac.	40 Ac.	80 Ac.	160 Ac.	b/d	b/d
0-1,000	18	28	—	—	21	39	74	129	238	20	10
1,000-1,500	27	37	57	97	21	39	74	129	238	40	10
1,500-2,000	36	46	66	106	21	39	74	129	238	40	10
2,000-3,000	45	55	75	115	22	41	78	135	249	60	20
3,000-4,000	54	64	84	124	23	44	84	144	265	80	20
4,000-5,000	63	73	93	133	24	48	93	158	288	100	25
5,000-6,000	72	82	102	142	26	52	102	171	310	120	25
6,000-7,000	81	91	111	151	28	57	111	184	331	140	30
7,000-8,000	91	101	121	161	31	62	121	198	353	160	30
8,000-8,500	103	113	133	173	34	68	133	215	380	180	35
8,500-9,000	112	122	142	182	36	74	142	229	402	180	35
9,000-9,500	127	137	157	197	40	81	157	250	435	200	35
9,500-10,000	152	162	182	222	43	88	172	272	471	200	35
10,000-10,500	190	210	230	270	48	96	192	300	515	210	35
10,500-11,000	—	225	245	285	—	106	212	329	562	225	35
11,000-11,500	—	255	275	315	—	119	237	365	621	255	35
11,500-12,000	—	290	310	350	—	131	262	401	679	290	35
12,000-12,500	—	330	350	390	—	144	287	436	735	330	35
12,500-13,000	—	375	395	435	—	156	312	471	789	375	35
13,000-13,500	—	425	445	485	—	169	337	506	843	425	35
13,500-14,000	—	480	500	540	—	181	362	543	905	480	35
14,000-14,500	—	540	560	600	—	200	400	600	1000	540	35

TABLE 2

Texas Offshore Allowables

Depth	1967 depth yardstick b/d		
	40 Ac.	80 Ac.	160 Ac.
0-2,000	200	330	590
2,000-3,000	220	360	640
3,000-4,000	245	400	705
4,000-5,000	275	445	785
5,000-6,000	305	490	865
6,000-7,000	340	545	950
7,000-8,000	380	605	1050
8,000-9,000	420	665	1150
9,000-10,000	465	730	1260
10,000-11,000	515	800	1380
11,000-12,000	565	875	1500
12,000-13,000	620	950	1625
13,000-14,000	675	1030	1750
14,000-15,000	735	1115	1880

Discovery Allowables:

1. Onshore—Extended from 18 months to 24 months. (Effective 3-28-66)
2. Onshore—Extended from 5 wells to 10 wells. (Effective 5-31-66)
3. Offshore discovery allowable is still limited to the 5 well and 18 month restriction.

Suggested minimum spacing for various units (Railroad Commission)

These figures are based on a rectangular shape with a length not more than twice the width and a well on the center line of adjacent units.

20 ac. = 330' × 993'
40 ac. = 467' × 933' (Statewide =
80 ac. = 660' × 1320'   467' × 1200')
160 ac. = 933' × 1867'
320 ac. = 1320' × 2640'
640 ac. = 1867' × 3735'

Appendix B

Answer to Problem 1, Chapter 5

Successful Prospect
Net Cash Flow

Year	AFIT investment $M	Net Income $M	Net Cash flow $M	Cumulative net cash flow—$M
0	−200	—	−200	−200
1	−50	—	−50	−250
2	−55	—	−55	−305
3	−195	—	−195	−500
4	−900	300	−600	−1,100← Maximum neg. cash flow
5	−100	500	+400	−700
6		500	500	−200
7		500	500	+300← Cash flow becomes pos.
8		500	500	800
9		500	500	1,300
10		500	500	1,800
11		500	500	2,300
12		500	500	2,800
13		300	300	3,100
14		300	300	3,400
15		100	100	3,500

Maximum negative cash flow in year 4

Cumulative cash flow becomes positive during year 7

Payout in year 7

Total after-tax investment: $1,500M

Actual value profit: $3,500M

Answer to Problem 1, Chapter 5

Investment Cash Flow Stream, $M

	1	2	3	4	5 Total col. 3 & 4	6 FIT Cr.	7 AFIT Inv.		
Yr.	Cap.	Tang.	Intang.	Exp.				Yr.	Remarks
0	200						200	0	Lease bonus
							200		total, year 0
1	40			10	10	5	45	1	Seismic work
				10	10	5	5		lease rental
							50		total, year 1
2	50						50	2	Add. lease bonus
				10	10	5	5		lease rental
							55		total, year 2
3		90	210		210	105	195	3	Discovery well
							195		total, year 3
4		400	600		600	300	700	4	Dev. well
		200					200		lease facilities
							900		total, year 4
5				200	200	100	100	5	Dry hole
							100		total, year 5

(3) + (4) = (5) $\longrightarrow$ (5) × .5 = (6) $\longrightarrow$ (1) + (2) + (3) + (4) − (6) = 1500
AFIT investment

$\uparrow$
Total AFIT investment
for this prospect

Answer to Problem 1, Chapter 6

10 doublings or roughly 73 years.

Answer to Problem 2, Chapter 6

| | Cash flow streams—AFIT | | | | Discounting the cash flow** | | | | | |
| | | | | | 15% | | 25% | | 30% | |
	Investment	Income	Net	Cumulative	Factors	Cash Flow	Factors	Cash Flow	Factors	Cash Flow
0	-200		-200	-200	1.00	-200	1.00	-200	1.00	-200
1	-900	200	-700	-900	0.90	-630	0.80	-560	0.75	-525
2	-100	300	200	-700	0.75	150	0.65	130	0.60	120
3		400	400	-300 *	0.65	260	0.50	200	0.45	180
4		400	400	+100	0.55	220	0.40	160	0.35	140
5		300	300	400	0.50	150	0.33	100	0.25	75
6		300	300	700	0.45	135	0.30	90	0.20	60
7		200	200	900	0.40	80	0.24	48	0.16	32
8		100	100	1,000	0.35	35	0.18	18	0.12	12
9		100	100	1,100	0.30	30	0.14	14	0.09	9
Total	-1,200	2,300	1,100	↑ Actual Value Profit		+230		-0-		-97

* Payout = 3.75 years

Maximum negative cash flow = -900

DCFR = 25%

**Discounted factors rounded

Answer To Problem 1, Chapter 7

1. The DCFR for development wells for the School prospect is over 100%. (Few computer programs show DCFR values beyond 100%.)
2. With a DCFR of over 100% the multiple for the development well DCFR is greater than four (the DCFR for the prospect being 24.5%).

Answer to Problem 2, Chapter 7

Investment Yardsticks

Using the cash flow streams shown below, determine the following:

(a) Actual Value Profit: (AFIT NCF = $1,310)
(b) Payout Period: (3 + 100/270 = 3.4)
(c) Ultimate Net Income Ratio: (1,310/640 = 2.1)
(d) Profit-to-BFIT Investment Ratio: (1,310/1,400 = .94)
(e) 14% PVP/AFIT I (Net Effective) Ratio: (370/934 = 0.40)
(f) Knowing that the 14%, 20% and 30% PVP values are $370M, $183M, and −$42M, respectively, plot a present value profile and determine the Discounted Cash Flow Rate:

(ANSWER FROM PLOT, DCFR = 28%)

Time Period	BFIT Investment	AFIT Investment	AFIT Cash Inflow	AFIT Net Cash Inflow
0	900	530	0	(530) ⎱ (640)
1	500	404	350	(110) ⎰
2			250	250
3			290	290
4			270	270
5			260	260
6			250	250
7			210	210
8			180	180
9			160	160
10			80	80
Totals:	1,400	934	2,300	1,310

Answer to Problem 3, Chapter 7

Investment Yardsticks

List the project(s) which would be optimum or acceptable under the following conditions. (Assume your company's cost of capital is 10% and you have no other investment opportunities unless otherwise noted):

A. Capital limited to a total $6,000M Investment budget.
    Projects: B-U-Y-I-T-N-W   Investment = 6,000
    10% PVP = 1,803
B. Capital limited to a total of $3,500M, your cost of capital is 15%, and Project T must be withdrawn because of political issues.
    Projects: U-B-O   Investment = 3,000   15% PVP = 460
    Project W (only other $500M inv. opportunity) has PV loss at 15% and is not attractive.
    Put unspent $500M capital in bank to draw interest.
C. No limit on capital resources but your cost of capital is 10%. All projects are acceptable since 10% PVP>0.
D. Your spouse (51% owner of the company) issues an edict that no projects having a 10% PVP/AFIT Investment ratio less than 0.35 can be initiated.
             Projects T (PVP/I = 208/500 = .416) and
    W (PVP/I = $\frac{188}{500}$ = .376 only acceptable projects.
E. You have only projects T & U which are mutually exclusive. You are capital limited with other reinvestment opportunities having a 10% PVP/I ratio equal to:
    (a) 0.5   (b) 0.35   (c) 0.25
    Neither acceptable   Project T   Project T
    What if T & U were not mutually exclusive? (a), (b), (c), conditions above
    (a) Neither   (b) Project T only   (c) Both T & U
                    (Project U = PVP/I = .323)
F. Your budget is cut to $1,000M and your cost of capital is
    (a) 5% T & W   (b) 10% T & W   (c) 15% U
    5% PVP = 1,005   10% PVP = 396   15% PVP = 217
G. You decide to rank the project in order of liquidity and take the four most attractive. (Payout is considered a measure of liquidity.)
    Projects O-U-B-Y would be optimum.

Answer to Problem 1, Chapter 10

    $-0.05 per roll.

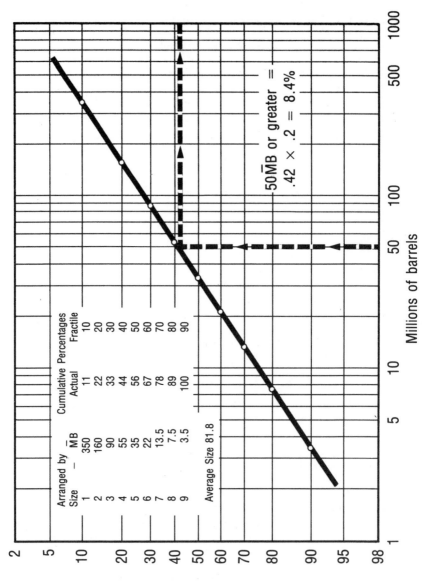

Answer to Problem 9-1: A field size distribution

Answer to Problems 1, 2, 3, Chapter 12

Sensitivity Checks
School Prospects
(Thousands of Dollars)

| | Base Case Cash Flows, AFIT | | | | Case 2: 2 × Expl. Expenditures | | |
| | | | | | | Discounted* | |
Year	Investment*	Income	Net		NCF	10%	15%
0	-500		-500		-1000	-1000	-1000
1	-232		-232		-464	-422	-367
2	-792		-792		-1584	-1309	-1198
3	-799		-799		-1598	-1120	-1051
4	-1841	1548	-293		-293	-200	-168
5	-628	1582	954		954	592	474
6		1622	1622		1622	916	701
7		1605	1605		1605	824	603
8		1593	1593		1593	743	521
9		783	783		783	332	223
10		783	783		783	302	194
11		768	768		768	269	165
12		753	753		753	240	141
13		753	753		753	218	122
Total	-4792	11790	6998		4675	385	-640
	DCFR = 24.5%					DCFR = 11.9%	

* Years 0-3 = Exploration expenditures

Sensitivity Checks
School Prospects
(Thousands of Dollars)

| | Case 3: 2 × Dev. Expend. NCF | | | Case 4: 2-Year Revenue Delay NCF | | |
| | AFIT | Discounted | | AFIT | Discounted* | |
Year	AFIT	10%	15%	AFIT	10%	18%
0	− 500	− 500	− 500	− 500	− 500	− 500
1	− 232	− 227	− 201	− 232	− 227	− 197
2	− 792	− 654	− 521	− 792	− 654	− 569
3	− 799	− 600	− 525	− 799	− 600	− 486
4	−2134	−1457	−1220	−1841	−1257	− 950
5	326	202	162	− 628	− 390	− 275
6	1622	915	701	1548	873	573
7	1605	823	603	1582	812	497
8	1593	744	521	1622	757	432
9	783	332	223	1605	681	362
10	783	302	194	1593	614	304
11	768	269	165	783	274	127
12	753	240	141	783	249	107
13	753	218	122	768	222	89
14				753	198	74
15				753	180	63
Total	**4529**	**607**	**− 135**	**6998**	**1232**	**−349**

DCFR = 14.1%

DCFR = 16.2%

*Years 0-3 = Exploration Expenditures

Answer to Problem 12–4: Graphic solution, DCFR, 2 × development expenditures

Answer to Problem 12–5: South Florida option, working interest vs. farmout

Appendix C

In Chapter 6, p. 84, we spoke of the effect of variations in compounding frequency. At that time the relative effect of various compounding frequencies was not shown. A simple illustration follows which will demonstrate the effect of compounding. In Table 6–1, Chapter 6, the FV of 1 invested at 10% grew to 2.59 in 10 years. We shall use this basic relationship in our illustration. For convenience our money invested will be $1000. Then:

$1000 invested at 10% compounded annually grows to $2,594 in 10 years.

It is a simple matter to show the effect of more frequent compounding. One can use standard interest tables. Usually the column heading in interest tables will be amount of 1. You must look in different sections, however, to get the right answer.

$1000 at 10% compounded semiannually for 10 years is in reality the same as $1,000 at 5% compounded annually for 20 years.

Look at the 5% interest table for 20 periods and you have $2,653. Therefore,

$1,000 invested at 10% compounded semiannually (5%—20 periods) grows to $2,653 in 10 years.

For quarterly compounding, use 2½% and 40 periods:

The answer is $2,685.

For monthly compounding (0.8⅓% and 120 periods):

$1000 at 10% for 10 years grows to $2,707.

Let's check the effect of more frequent compounding. The net effect of even monthly compounding is $113 in 10 years. The additional interest comes in over the entire ten years with most in the latter years. The $113 is 4% more than the total money after annual compounding.

As discussed in Chapters 5 and 9, the dominance of several key parameters relegates small differences (such as income from more frequent compounding) to insignificance.

Appendix **D**

One of our goals was to illustrate without the computer. Since a Monte Carlo simulation requires a computer, this section is relegated to an appendix. As was the case in the two chapters on risk analysis, it draws from many sources, but in particular from unpublished work of G. Rogge Marsh.[1] The basic concepts involving Monte Carlo simulation are not new and can be found in most recent textbooks on statistics.

The term "Monte Carlo analysis" was spawned by two mathematicians, John von Neumann and S. Ulam. They developed the technique to solve a problem on nuclear shielding which was too complex for analytical solution and too risky for empirical solution.[2]

What Monte Carlo Simulation Does

In Monte Carlo simulation, a specific operation is mathematically performed thousands of times.

Input data involve estimates of the range of probabilities for the variables. By means of a random number generator, specific values for each variable are chosen at frequencies described by input data. Values for each variable are generated and the resultant answer to the mathematical operations contains the complete range of probable solutions. The answer takes the form of a cumulative probability distribution curve.

We will now backtrack a bit and explain more thoroughly some of the terms.

Random Numbers

First let's explain a random number generator and why we want to use one. Remember our 27 case tree diagram, Fig. 10–1. It showed 27 possible combinations of three values for three parameters; but there are really more than 27 possibilities. What is more, we may not have made the best combination of the various values. If not, would

1,000 cases give a different or better answer? Whenever we have problems involving many combinations of variables Monte Carlo simulation is useful. It will show us the most probable answer based on a sufficient quantity of cases to test the limits of all variables.

Most computers have a subroutine which will generate random numbers. (You could think of the last two digits in a column of telephone numbers as a random number generator.) Numbers are selected between 0 and 1.0 and related to the input data which is submitted in the form of a frequency distribution. The computer converts the input data, a frequency distribution, into a cumulative probability distribution. The numbers chosen then relate to the cumulative probability; thus, although the number is randomly chosen, the frequency of occurrence represents a judgment by the geologist. The resultant values *do* reflect his estimate of the most probable occurrences.

The Input

The geologists' judgments enter the computer by means of frequency distributions. Remember, a frequency distribution is easily converted to a probability distribution. Often these distributions are no more than triangular distribution of the minimum, maximum, and most likely.

Fig. D–1 illustrates the probability distributions used for the School project. The three variables for each parameter, representing our minimum, maximum, and most likely, are shown by circles. Note carefully the following:

1. The three values used previously no longer represent the lowest or highest possible values. For example in recovery factors we assigned probabilities to values of 0.7, 1.0 and 1.5 $\overline{M}$cf/acre-ft. When these three points are placed in triangular distribution the minimum point becomes 0.4 $\overline{M}$cf/acre-ft. and the maximum point becomes 1.6 $\overline{M}$cf acre-ft. These points, on the X axis, are absolute. No value can be higher than 1.6 $\overline{M}$cf or lower than 0.4 $\overline{M}$cf/acre-ft.

2. Does the diagram on recovery factor help you see there are, within this triangular distribution, an infinite number of possibilities between 0.4 and 1.6 $\overline{M}$cf/acre-ft.?

3. Knowing that the computer converts these triangular distributions to cumulative probability distributions, does it also show you that, despite the many possible values, the geologists' estimates of probability are in control? No matter how many values are chosen by the computer, the probabilities established by the explorationist are

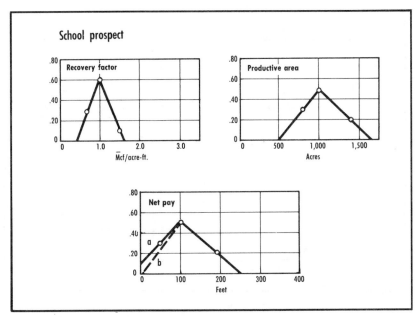

Fig. D–1 Probability distributions for field size

in command. The randomly selected cases will still show the highest probability around 1.0 $\overline{M}$cf/acre-ft.

4. The distributions do not have to be triangular. If triangular they do not have to be isosceles triangles, i.e., the most likely case does not have to be exactly halfway between the minimum and maximum. A rectangular distribution means you think there is no most likely value and that the minimum and maximum values have the same probability of occurrence. Distributions can be continuous—curved rather than triangular. They can be discrete, in which case the variables can have only certain distinct values. There is nothing magic about triangular distributions. They just result from three values and many explorationists think more easily in three-value terms. See Fig. D–2 for distribution examples.

5. Note the net pay diagram on Fig. D–1. The three probabilities used in Fig. 10–1 cause line a to intersect the Y axis. Mathematically this says we expect some negative values, an impossibility. (The minimum becomes − 25 ft.) The moral is this—if you plan to submit triangular distributions (based on probabilities other than maximum and minimum) to a computer, plot them first to make sure you are not assigning impossible values. Line b can be substituted with little

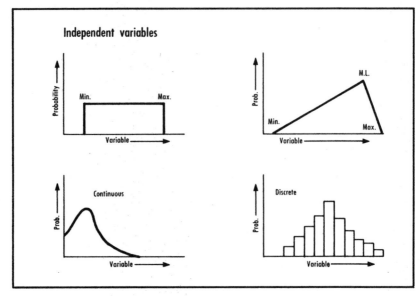

Fig. D–2 Types of distributions

change in end results. It is close to but not zero at the X axis and raises the 30% probability from 50 ft. to 60 ft.

The Output

The computer takes a random number for a variable, reads its probability of occurrence from the cumulative probability distribution created from data submitted. It reads corresponding values for each variable, multiplies them and computes one value for the answer desired. It then repeats this process many times—each time choosing a random number but relating it to the geologists' judgment as to what values were most probable.

Our triangular distributions for the School prospect were entered in a computer simulation program. In about 20 seconds 5,000 reserve size cases were computed. The output from the program was as follows:

Reserve-BCF	Probability
29.8	.261
50.4	.232
68.1	.203

Reserve-BCF	Probability
83.9	.174
100.0	.145
117.7	.116
138.8	.087
168.1	.058
208.0	.029
410.1	.001

The results are plotted on Fig. D–3 in the same manner as our 27 case example of Fig. 10–3. Note the smoothness from 5,000 cases compared to the 27. The distributions are similar however. The average reserve and risk weighted reserve are compared below for the two types of calculations.

	Hand calculation 27 cases	Computer run 5,000 cases
Average reserve	129	141
Risk weighted reserve	29.2	32.0

Fig. D–3   Cumulative probability distribution

The output from Monte Carlo simulation is in the form of a cumulative probability distribution for the desired answer. The case illustrated was reserve size.

Why Monte Carlo Simulation?

There are benefits from Monte Carlo simulation:

1. The frequency of occurrence of all critical variables can be handled simultaneously and randomly based on input judgment. The answer received is superior to a sensitivity check where only one variable can be tested at a time; however, you still may wish to test the sensitivity of one or more key variables separately.

2. The range of possible values derived from input probability distributions shows that you really have no such thing as a single most likely case. The steepest slope of the cumulative probability distribution is the most likely range of values. However, there are instances where the slope is never very steep. In such cases the range of yardsticks (DCF, PVP, etc.) may be broad at the higher frequencies. If this is true, you need to know this characteristic of your investment opportunity.

3. You will better describe an opportunity, learning more about the high side potential and the low side risks.

If you have a computer available, you may wish to explore this technique. It has interesting possibilities for those willing to take the time to understand its strengths and weaknesses.

BIBLIOGRAPHY

1. Marsh, G. Rogge, "Risk Assessment Terminology," 1970 unpublished paper.
2. Springer, Clifford H. et. al, "Probabilistic Models," Vol. 4 of the Mathematics for Management Series 1968, Richard D. Irwin, Inc., p. 135.

Appendix **E**

You may sometimes be faced with the need to discount a cash flow but not have any discount tables or a computer handy. Here's a shortcut method to establish a PVP by discounting a cash flow without tables—a desk calculator is required, however.

The Method With Tables

For our basic data, we shall use a short cash flow for five years.

Discounting with 10% Factors

Year	Net cash flow—$M̄	Discount factors 10%	Discounted cash flow—$M̄ @ 10%
1	100	.909	91
2	100	.826	83
3	100	.751	75
4	100	.683	68
5	100	.621	62
	500		379

With the 10% discount factors, the present value of the income stream is shown to be $379 million.

The Shortcut—Sans Tables

The shortcut method involves only the first year discount factor— which is

$$\frac{1}{(1 + i)^1} \text{ or } \frac{1}{(1 + i)}$$

In the case of 10% tables, this number is:

$$\frac{1}{1 + 0.1} = \frac{1}{1.1} = 0.909$$

To apply the shortcut, start at the year of the final cash flow (year 5 in our case) and calculate as follows: multiply income in last year times the first year factor, add the next earlier year's income, multiply by the same factor, etc. until last year (1) has been added and multiplied. A sample calculation follows.

Shortcut Discounting Method

Year	Net cash flow, $\overline{M}$		Order of calculation
1	100	$100 + 317 = 417 \times .909 = 379$	Step 5
2	100	$100 + 249 = 349 \times .909 = 317$	Step 4
3	100	$100 + 174 = 274 \times .909 = 249$	Step 3
4	100	$100 + 91 = 191 \times .909 = 174$	Step 2
5	100	$100 \times .909 = 91$	Step 1

The result is exactly the same as having all of the discount factors—$379 million. Leave the proof to the mathematicians. The method works.

Appendix F

The Growth of an IRA

Given:

Annual Contribution = $2000
Annual Compound Interest Rate = 10%

Basic Formula:

$$FV = I \frac{(1 + i)^n - 1}{i}$$

where:

FV = future value of a series of annual investments
I = annual investment
i = Interest Rate
n = number of years compounded at i

Sample Calculation:

$$FV = 2000 \frac{(1 + 0.1)^{10} - 1}{0.1} = 2000 \frac{2.59 - 1}{0.1} = 2000 \,(15.9)$$

$$= \$31,800$$

Growth of an IRA		
n	Your Contribution	FV of IRA
10	$20,000	$ 31,800
20	40,000	114,550
30	60,000	328,988
40	80,000	885,185

FV's BFIT (Tax Paid When Withdrawn)

This formula and the illustration (calculation) of a $2,000 annual IRA, show the power of money to grow, through compound interest. At 10%, an annual IRA of $2,000 would cost you $80,000, but your account would be worth $885,185 after 40 years! (Subject to income limits in 1988).

Acronyms

ACRS accelerated cost recovery system
AFIT after Federal income tax
AOFP absolute open flow potential
AVP actual value profit

BFIT before Federal income tax
BPCL base production control level

DCFR discounted cash flow rate
DCQ daily contract quantity
DOE Department of Energy

EIS environmental impact statement
ERA Energy Regulatory Agency

FERC Federal Energy Regulatory Commission
FPC Federal Power Commission
FSD field size distribution
FV future value

GRR growth rate of return

IDC intangible development costs
ITC investment tax credit
IRS Internal Revenue Service

LNG liquified natural gas

MER maximum efficient rate (of production)
MIRR modified internal rate of return
MMS Minerals Managment Service
MROR minimum rate of return

NEPA   National Environmental Protection Agency
NGPA   Natural Gas Policy Act
NPX   discovery allowable (Texas)

OSHA   Office of Safety and Health Administration

P/I   profit to investment ratio
PV   present value
PVP   present value profit
PVP/I   present value profit divided by the investment

RRC   Railroad Commission (Texas)

SNG   synthetic natural gas
SYD   sum-of-the-years digits

TZA   top zone allowable

UNIR   ultimate net income ratio

WI   working interest

Glossary

Absolute Open Flow Potential

A theoretical value calculated upon initial completion of a gas well.

Accelerated Income Investment

An investment made primarily to obtain an advantage in timing of income. Implies no increase in ultimate recovery but with recovery greater in earlier and reduced project life. Results in present value profit but actual value loss.

Accounting Procedure

Matches book outlays against revenue as produced. It provides the effect of a proposal on overall corporate book financial results and also reporting corporate earning power to the shareholders.

Actual Value Profit

The total cumulative net cash flow on a project at its conclusion.

Ad Valorem Taxes

A state or county tax assessed upon the value of a property.

Allowable Allocation Formulae

Methods for dividing the total allowable of an oil or gas reservoir among the operators of the various leases in a manner considered equitable.

Allowable Depletion

The amount of depletion that may be claimed as an expense in a given year. The greater of cost or percentage depletion.

Associated Gas Well Allowables

A ruling that provides relief for operators of gas-cap acreage. Permits withdrawal of reservoir volume of gas equivalent to oil allowable. Sometimes reclassified as non-associated reservoirs upon decline of oil production.

Average Book Net Income

Net profit (or loss) as reported to the stockholders.

Book Investment

Those items capitalized on the corporate books.

Book Rate of Return

Cumulative booked net income (profit) divided by summation of the average annual booked investments.

Budget

The allocation of money for expense and capital purposes.

Capital

Expenditures that may not be completely deducted from income in the year in which they are made (e.g. office equipment, automobiles, cost of leases, etc.).

Cash Flow Analysis

A procedure matching cash outflows against cash inflows when disbursements are made or cash received. It provides the basis necessary to develop yardsticks essential to evaluating or comparing investment opportunities.

Cash Flow Stream

An economic model of the inflow and outflow of all related funds over the life of an investment opportunity.

Composite Risk Factor

The geologist's informed assignment of a number that represents the probability that a given wildcat will result in a producing well. Also called the chance of success.

Corporate Books

The method of accounting employed for reporting financial experience of a company to management and stockholders.

Cost Depletion

A depletion allowance based on the cost of a mineral property.

Daily Contract Quantity

The daily amount of gas that, by contract, will be taken—based usually on reserves. Example: 1 Mcf/Day per 8 Bcf of reserve.

Depletion

A reduction of income reflecting the exhaustion of a mineral deposit by extraction of the minerals.

Depreciation

A reduction of income reflecting the loss in useful value of a capitalized (or tangible) equipment by reason of wear and tear.

Straight-Line Depreciation. A method of computing by dividing the depreciable amount into equal annual parts based on the life of the equipment or based on a fixed time schedule issued by a taxing agency.

Accelerated Depreciation. A method of assigning a greater percentage of depreciable investment to the earlier years of the life of the equipment.

Sum-of-the-Years Digits. A method applicable to new equipment placed in service prior to 1981. It multiplies the depreciable cost each year by a SYD fraction. The numerator is the remaining life of the equipment (or assigned life) at the beginning of the year, and the denominator is the sum of the digits in the overall life (actual or assigned) of the equipment.

Declining Balance. A method whereby the annual depreciation is computed at either 150% or 200% of the straight-line depreciation rate. The 150% factor is applicable to equipment in used condition and the 200% for new equipment.

Accelerated Cost Recovery System. A method of assigning depreciation based on a rate set by Federal tax laws and an assigned life, also set by Federal tax laws.

Unit of Production Depreciation. A method used for calculating depreciation on lease and well equipment whose service life is largely controlled by the physical depletion of reserves.

Depth Yardsticks

A table of allowables established by state regulatory bodies for statewide application to oil completions. The allowables normally increase with increased depth and spacing.

Direct Operating Expenses

Costs identified with a unit of output (pumper and gang salaries, repair and maintenance of lease facilities, etc.).

Discounted Cash Flow Rate

The discount rate at which a discounted cash flow stream equals zero.

District Overhead

Expenses applicable to operations but which cannot be attributed directly to a specific lease or property. Overhead is allocated on some consistent basis.

Dry Hole Deeper Drilling Costs

Dry hole costs (losses) below the deepest producing zone.

Employee Welfare

Benefit expenditures deducted from income. They include vacation time, sick leave, contributions to medical plans, etc.

Exempt Allowables

Not subject to proration. (Scheduled allowable is the same as the calendar day allowable.)

Discovery Allowable (NPX). High producing rate permitted for first wells in a reservoir for various lengths of time, as determined by various states or in the Outer Continental Shelf by Federal government agencies.

Marginal Allowable (M). An Allowable to prevent premature abandonment of economically marginal wells.

Others (X). Allowables granted for various reasons.

Expense

Expenditures that are deducted from income in the year in which they are made.

Federal Energy Regulatory Commission (Formerly Federal Power Commission)

An agency regulating interstate transportation and sale of natural gas "for the protection of consumers." It administers the regulations associated with the Natural Gas Policy Act which include price regulations for certain categories of natural gas, both intrastate and interstate.

Field (Common Terminology)

The general area underlaid by one or more reservoirs formed by a common structural or stratigraphic feature.

Field (Railroad Commission Designation)

When referring to all reservoirs, the same as the common terminology. It also is used by the RRC to refer to a single reservoir.

Field Rules

Rules set forth to ensure orderly development and exploitation in a specific field. May apply to one, several or all reservoirs in a field. Usually include spacing rules, allowable allocation formulae, gas-oil ratio limit, surface casing requirement. May include many special or unique provisions. Normally requested by one or more operators in an open hearing.

Field Size Distribution

A cumulative distribution of field sizes in a play, trend or basin, usually shown on logprobability graph paper. A straight line on such paper indicates a lognormal distribution.

Future Value

The value of a single investment or a series of future annual cash flows compounded at a given interest rate to a specific year.

Growth Rate of Return

A percentage calculated based on a target year, to which annual positive investments are either compounded or discounted at a given interest rate. Negative cash flows are discounted to year zero and represent an inferred investment.

Incremental Economics

As used in investment evaluation, the term "incremental" usually refers to the algebraic difference (per time period) between two cash flow streams.

Intangible Development Costs
The portion of drilling costs that has no salvage value.

Investment Tax Credit
A credit to (deduction from) income based on a percentage specified by applicable tax laws.

Investment
For *accounting purposes,* investment includes those items that are capitalized.

As used in *investment evaulation* it refers to any expenditure made in the expectation that increased profits will result. The after-tax value is commonly used for yardstick purposes; however, other concepts can be used (such as the discounted negative cash flows used in the GRR yardstick).

Investment Yardsticks
Criteria used to help in measuring, comparing and describing investment opportunities.

Investor's Interest Rate (IIR)
The same as the discounted cash flow rate.

Lease Bonus
A cash payment for a lease on a property. The bonus is the lessee's cost in the property and must be capitalized.

Lease Rentals
A sum paid, usually annually, during the term of the lease for the privilege of deferring development of the property. Sometimes called delay rentals. Lease rentals are expensed.

Maximum Efficient Rate
The highest rate of production that will prevent waste or loss of future production.

Maximum Negative Cash Flow
The greatest amount of money (on an annual basis) out-of-pocket at any one time.

Modified Internal Rate of Return
A percentage yardstick that compensates for sign reversals in cash flow streams. After the first reversal (switching from negative cash flows to positive or vice versa) additional reversals cause additional roots (percentages), obviously confusing to the analyst. The MIRR produces only one root, regardless of the number of sign reversals.

Minerals Management Service
A branch of the Department of the Interior that regulates sealed bid lease sales and other activities in the outer continental shelf of the U.S.

Minimum Rate of Return
The lowest discount rate that a company will allow for any investment. An investment not having a positive (greater than zero) cash flow at the minimum rate is considered unacceptable.

Mutually Exclusive
A group of alternate investments, only one of which may be finally accepted.

Net Interest
A company's portion of the gross income after deducting the royalty interest.

Non-Associated Gas Well Allowables
Allowables fixed at a percentage of adjusted open flow potential. Exceptions can normally be obtained in the late stages of depletion to prevent waste. The allowable is a fraction of total field nomination as determined by the allocation formula.

Payout Period
Time required for the total investment (AFIT) to be recovered from net cash flow. The point at which the cumulative net cash flow becomes positive. For some types of farmout, farmin or carried interest agreements the payout is figured on a BFIT basis.

Penalized Allowables
High Gas-Oil Ratio. Penalized for casinghead gas production in excess of gas-oil ratio limit to conserve reservoir energy.

Limited Capacity. Allowable fixed below top-zone allowable because of the inability to demonstrate productive capacity.

Percentage Depletion
A statutory allowance calculated on earnings rather than on the cost of a property. For certain small operators (less than 1,000 b/d production) it is based on 15% of the gross income from a property, but limited to 50% of the net income of the property.

Present Value Profile
A plot of present value profits (or losses) calculated by applying various discount rates to the net cash flow stream of an investment.

Present Value Profit
Today's worth of future profits at a given discount rate.

Production Taxes
State and municipal taxes levied on oil and gas products.

Profit-to-Investment Ratio
The ultimate actual value profit divided by the investment. The investment may be the after-tax investment, the capitalized investment, the total cash outlay, or the maximum negative cash flow.

Proration

Restriction of production, usually on the basis of market demand.

Proration Factor

Percentage of a well's scheduled allowable that is permitted to produce on a calendar basis. When prorationing was in effect the factor was adjusted monthly with changing supply and demand conditions.

Railroad Commission of Texas (RRC)

An administrative agency charged with the duty of making and enforcing rules to regulate the oil and gas producing industry in Texas.

Rank Wildcat

A well drilled in search of oil or gas on a prospect not previously productive. Implies a significant amount of geological and geophysical effort to define the prospect.

Revenue

Income from sale of raw material or products.

Risk

The possibility of loss stated in terms of the probability of various outcomes. Expressed as a percent chance of occurrence.

Risk-Weighted

This term used with reference to reserves or profits. The reserve is multiplied by its chance of occurrence to get the risk-weighted reserve. A profit is also multiplied by its chance of occurrence, but is added to the loss from the chance of the prospect not being productive.

Scheduled Allowable

Top zone or penalized allowable for a well. The total is used as a basis for controlling statewide production using proration factors where proration is in force.

Statewide Rules

A set of general rules applied to all fields (reservoirs) not specifically covered by field rules. Certain statewide rules apply to all fields, including those with field rules.

Tangible Costs

Items that have a salvage value. Must be capitalized.

Top Zone Allowable (TZA)

Maximum per well allowable granted to completions in a specific reservoir. Most often based on depth yardsticks, but with many exceptions.

Total Calendar Allowable

Scheduled allowable, subject to proration × proration factor + exempt allowable

Ultimate Net Income Ratio

A type of profit-to-investment ratio. The ultimate actual value profit divided by the maximum negative cash flow.

Well Spacing

Regulation of the number and location of wells completed in the same reservoir. Normally spacing is stated as minimum permissible distances from lease lines and between wells. It essentially forces each well to drain a specific number of productive acres (proration unit) within the operator's own lease.

Wildcat Risk

The probability that each of several geologic conditions, which are more or less independent of each other, will occur and result in a producing well.

Working Interest

A company's portion of gross income before reduction by royalty interest.

Index